Sam's Homecoming

Sam's Homecoming

A Story of a Soul's Search for Home

Tim Tengblad

Illustrations by William Beaupre

Pen & Publish
Saint Louis, Missouri

Published by Pen & Publish, LLC, USA

PEN & PUBLISH

www.PenandPublish.com
info@PenandPublish.com

Saint Louis, Missouri
(314) 827-6567

Paperback ISBN: 978-1-956897-87-6
Hardcover ISBN: 978-1-956897-88-3
ebook ISBN: 978-1-956897-89-0
Library of Congress Control Number: 2026942916

Cover and interior illustrations by William Beaupre (william-beaupre.com)

To all I have walked with through this life. You have shown me the Divine. You are my life. One and the same.

"We are all just walking each other home."

Ram Dass

Contents

Introduction

IN MY FIRST BOOK, *Remembering: A Pastor's Bridge to Spirituality Beyond the Church*, I told the fictional story of my meeting "Sam," and the conversations we shared about the nature of life, reality, and ourselves.

Sam was a seeker, walking in this world trying to find his way through the pain, challenges, and joys of his life.

As the title indicates, I was a Lutheran pastor for thirty-five years and loved so many aspects of ministry. But after twenty-nine years, I began to follow an inner voice that was telling me, "There's more." More than what the Church, and I, had been telling people.

So I, too, became a seeker, and in *Remembering*, I share with Sam where the inner voice had led me—to go within, and remember what my soul already knew:

- Natural oneness with the Divine, everyone, and everything.
- Love is the deepest Truth of ourselves and reality.

In writing *Sam's Homecoming*, I came to know Sam's backstory, and the new life he set out to live. I have truly enjoyed listening to his story, writing it down, and now sharing it with you. There were many surprises for me—people, experiences, and responses I didn't see coming.

And through it all, his story brought me to the place where all of our stories end.

I wish you well on your walk with Sam Crawford, and his golden Shadow.

You are love,

Tim

1

Homeward Bound

SAM CRAWFORD WAS ONCE AGAIN turning to his Toyota RAV4 to help him move on. Whatever the destination, it had always been faithful to him. Even taking him where he did not want to go—to an empty apartment—three long years ago.

As he drove away from his home that day, the second of two horrible days in his life, the RAV4's rearview mirror relentlessly reminded him of the life he had built with his soon-to-be ex-wife, Jadyn. Now in late June of 2025, the car's rearview mirror was doing its thing again. Yes. The RAV was consistent. Reliable. Trustworthy. It knew its purpose. Everything Sam wished he was more of.

Sam had named it Charlie, after Charlie Finnegan, who had been his best friend growing up.

Charlie moved to his town just before the start of second grade. Since the first day, when Charlie was the only one who laughed at a joke Sam told, they were inseparable. Sam could always count on Charlie for a laugh, companionship, and comfort. For . . . whatever he needed at the time.

The funny thing about Sam and Charlie was that they always seemed to know what the other was going to say or do. They finished each other's sentences. They played basketball together, and the rhythm they knew carried over to the court. In a playoff game their junior year against their biggest rival, the score was tied with seven seconds left.

Despite the plan drawn up during the time-out, Sam Crawford let his intuition coach him. When play started, Sam anticipated and intercepted a crosscourt pass. He had nothing but open court in front of him. With the crowd now standing and roaring, Sam drove downcourt to their basket. As he started to go up for the layup, he saw the defender coming into position to block his shot. He knew Charlie would be coming up behind him. Without even looking back, he dropped a bounce pass around his right hip to Charlie. Sam knew when the crowd erupted that Charlie had finished his sentence. Again.

From that day on, whenever Sam needed him, there was Charlie behind him, telling him in one way or another, "I'm right behind you." Until that horrible day when he couldn't be anymore. Now he was trusting Charlie again. Charlie RAV4. This time to take him and his new best friend to Newcastle, a much larger city about ninety minutes away from his old life in Brayden.

A growing friendship with his intuition had begun about a year ago. The more Sam listened to its wisdom, the more he discovered it could be trusted. He had learned that it not only had his best interest in mind, but also knew what it was. And now it was telling him he needed the "New" in Newcastle. He needed a fresh start. This time as a TV talk show host at a startup TV station, KLUV, in Newcastle.

Yes, that's right. This former high school physics teacher was once again driving downcourt. This time toward a totally crazy career change. It was a dream he had long kept to himself. A dream that paid him a visit once in a while, but not for some time. Now it was back, courtesy of a college friend, Heather Bedford.

She and Sam met their spouses there, and the two couples continued to get together a couple of times a year. Heather had always seen something in Sam. Something he often didn't see in himself. So, when she got her new job as KLUV's general manager, she called Sam, and began "talking crazy" to him. At least that was Sam's take on it. She told him about a group of eight highly successful women entrepreneurs. They had obtained a license from the FCC to start a television station. Their vision for programming was clear.

KLUV ~ Lifting Up the Human Spirit ~

In the summer of 2025, the country was coming apart at the seams. Torn by fear, division, anger, and chaos. Most everyone lost in their labels of red and blue. Right and Left. Conservative and liberal.

Religion seemed to only make it worse, with Christians wrapping Jesus up in the swaddling clothes of the American flag. Christian nationalism and patriotism were one and the same for an increasing number of clarity-seeking souls. Families torn apart over who would or would not pledge their allegiance to one man, who some saw as a deity, or at least its messenger.

People were increasingly tuning out. Turning less to their televisions for their connection with the world, and more to the echo chambers of their chosen social media. For many, television was at best a distraction. A means to distract themselves from themselves. To escape through entertainment. And the choices often reflected the very thing they wished to escape. While decrying the increased violence all around them, yet another show would emerge with people pointing guns at each other.

In the midst of all of this, these gifted women had a different vision of television. They saw television as a way *through* it all, and not only as an escape. They wanted to create a platform that would counter the violence found in "entertainment." They found most of the news and political commentary shows were only *increasing* the divisions of society, causing those in either encampment to pound the stakes of their tents even deeper.

They were well aware of the general population's fatigue and despair over the current climate. They themselves were exhausted with it all, and their research clearly showed there was a *growing* number out there who felt the same.

They were investing in a new kind of station that would inspire people to do positive things, and bring people together. One that would raise up hope, while not ignoring the realities of the world.

Despite the research, it was still a huge gamble. Stations still worked from the old paradigm that fear, violence, and drama sell. No one had put big money on an entire station with this kind of vision. No one had put it all on the line for hope. For inclusion instead of exclusion. For love instead of fear. Thus the call letters, KLUV.

At Heather's invitation, Sam drove to Newcastle one weekend in January to learn more. He immediately loved the vision, and found it resonating perfectly with the direction his life had taken since last summer. But he still was totally stunned when Heather made him an offer to host his own show.

"Why me, Heather? I've never done anything like this."

"Sam, I know you. You're a communicator. You're smart. Articulate. Kind. Empathetic. You listen. You have a good heart. You will come across well to our viewers."

Heather could see a certain intrigue in Sam's eyes, but knew something was causing concern. "What is it, Sam?"

"I've got to admit, Heather. This is really attractive to me," Sam said, as he turned to look out her office window. "But after the divorce, things are shaky. I'm still trying to figure this all out financially. Child support and all. It's tough to think about giving up my teaching position."

"You wouldn't have to totally give it up, Sam. What about taking a sabbatical year and trying it out? You could make more money, and you can always go back if it's not working out. But I think it will."

Sam looked out the window again and pondered. It was a long ponder. It brought Heather back to their college days. She knew Sam was prone to go off somewhere during a conversation.

He nodded, as if he was reassuring himself. "Sabbatical. Yeah. That feels . . . peaceful. Right."

Heather smiled as she leaned forward. "The investors are incredible. So smart, and they know what they want. Among so many other things, they're diverse—White, Black, Asian, Latina. They want the programming to be diverse and inclusive. I know that's important to you. Individually, almost everything they've touched has turned to gold. So they come with deep pockets. Eight. Deep. Pockets.

"In our phone calls, you spoke of a spiritual awakening you started having last summer. 'Remembering,' I believe you called it? And with these investors, they're deeply spiritual. They would like spirituality to be the underlying foundation of a Sunday morning show they have in mind. That made me want to talk with you all the more. We'll just need to be careful how we do it, so your show is as inclusive as possible.

"They're smart with their money, so of course they've hired the best researchers. Generally, more women than men gravitate toward the spiritual. They're the ones who are initially going to be attracted to your show.

"Women are interested in intelligent, thoughtful, heartfelt content. They want depth. They demand to be respected, and they can smell it a mile away when they're not. With you hosting the show, and having a majority of your guests being women, we believe we can both appeal to those women, and—"

"Bring in the male demographic," Sam said.

"Ooh. Listen to you, Sam Crawford. Already talking demographics!

"The investors are fine with you focusing only on your weekly show the first couple of months or so. Just to give you some time to study the business. The craft. Get your feet wet, and for our audience to get to know you. Then we'd like to get you involved with some feature stories."

It was then that Heather knew that Sam Crawford had left the building. He looked out the window a second time, and saw himself fishing. Feeling the pull on his line, and comparing it to the pull of his soul he was now feeling. He could feel his energy rising. He quickly knew his soul wanted to take the bait. He extended his hand for a good old-fashioned "seal the deal" handshake. Sam Crawford had big hands. It served him well holding a basketball, or a Big Mac. He smiled and said, "Your vision. I'm right behind you."

Everything was so exciting, sure, and positive at their meeting, and in the conversations that followed. But now a growing sense of doubt was flooding into him as each passing mile brought him closer to Newcastle. To reality.

"This is crazy!" he told his traveling companion. "What was she thinking? What am *I* thinking?"

She looked into Sam's eyes in the rearview mirror, and recognized the look of being lost. With the unfamiliar scenery passing by, she felt it match her own. But there was a familiar feeling too. She could always feel what was driving this one who responded to the sound of "Sam." She felt what drove him to New Beginnings Rescue that first day she met him.

When Sam walked through the rescue that day, nothing felt right, until it did. He spotted a golden retriever, lying in the far corner of a large, crowded, caged area. She was turned away from Sam. A position he somehow knew she had been in for a while.

Sam felt something resonate and couldn't turn away. When she finally turned, and her eyes met Sam's, they both knew they shared a new beginning. One that the intuition of their hearts had been sharing for some time.

In spite of that telling first gaze, she was very slow to move toward Sam, who gave her the time and space she needed. Being a big man, he sat down on the floor, and just kept smiling at her. "What's her name?" he asked a staff person. "We don't know. A farmer spotted her by the side of the road, tied to a tree. No tags. Nothing. No one has come. It's been three weeks. We're running out of time."

When she felt safe enough, she got up. Slowly putting one paw in front of the other. Never taking her eyes off of Sam. A walk that reminded Sam of his early days after the separation. One foot in front of the other. One breath, and then another. The first days of living alone, not seeing his kids every day, and in need of his own rescue.

Eventually, she got close enough for Sam to reach out and touch her. She surprised herself that she let him do that. But she could sense that something felt different now. She looked again into Sam's eyes, and whatever that was resonated again within them both. It was like an inner tuning fork was struck. A pitch-perfect kind of peace, telling her, "All is well."

When she got close enough for Sam to gently touch her, Sam gazed into eyes that he knew were looking for something. "Hey, girl. How 'bout we bring each other home?"

No sooner had the words left his mouth, and Sam knew the name he would give her. Shadow. He saw the movie *Homeward Bound: The Incredible Journey* as a kid and loved it. The story of a lost golden retriever traveling long distances, looking for and miraculously finding her way back home. It was as if Sam Crawford saw in her, his Shadow. They would be perfect for each other. Two beings trying to find their way home.

As Charlie drove them home that day, Sam's heart ached as she looked back at New Beginnings Rescue. Her whimper reminding him that leaving wasn't new territory for either of them.

"Oh, it's okay, girl. It's going to be okay . . . I think."

When she walked into Sam's sparse apartment that first day of their new beginning, whatever it was she was looking and hoping for, this wasn't it. There was a certain smell or taste in the air. It was like she could taste the recipe, the mix of contradictions that Sam had been using for the life he had served up for the both of them:

> *Despair mixed with bitter disappointment. Add some self-loathing to some regret. Mix one measure of hope with two of hopelessness. To the loneliness, add a desire to be alone. Try and forgive what seemed unforgivable. Try and love what saw itself as unlovable.*

Sam had followed his own directions.

> *Stir. Let sit for two years. Serves one golden retriever, and one divorced teacher who eats alone, far too often.*

One golden who had every right to wonder in those first days if she really had been rescued.

It didn't take long, however, for Shadow to add one essential ingredient that changed the taste of everything. Oxytocin. Through one shared look into each other's eyes, this chemical elixir of bonding that she was so good at cooking up, raised up feelings of love, trust, empathy, and connection. It became their mutual Charlie. Dependable. Trustworthy.

She didn't really know what it was, but she did know it to be a dog's superpower. And Shadow clearly loved being a dog. She loved her walks together with Sam. When they'd get out on a favorite trail, she loved to run ahead of Sam as fast as she could. She'd turn around when she feared she couldn't see Sam anymore, and run back to him so fast that she couldn't stop when she got to him, and ran through his legs. Then she'd run past him to do it all over again.

Shadow had her own need of Sam. Her own story, and Sam didn't know the half of it. There was that very slight "hitch in her giddyup" that Sam always wondered about. No one at New Beginnings Rescue could tell him the "why" of it.

But then came last summer, and she started to notice something going on with Sam. Something delicious was added to the recipe. She started to sense Sam's increasing peace. Before, when Sam would give her a hug, she felt a desperate, "I need you." That summer, Sam's hug felt more like a contented, "I love you." He was smiling more. Or as Shadow would probably put it, smiling *again.* Somehow she knew that smile had always been there. Waiting to come out and play with her.

Last summer turned into a beautiful one for her in other ways. She didn't know why, but Sam was no longer leaving most mornings. She hated it when Sam left. Being left was the salt that always knew how to find and torment her deepest wounds.

With Sam around more, and seeming in no hurry to go anywhere, she came to love just lying beside him. Just the two of them. Together. It felt safe to let go, and in the letting go she would have the most exciting dreams. In her adventures, she was always running and chasing something that she knew she once had, but had now lost sight of. It didn't really matter though, because she'd wake up and find it again in Sam.

Sam would watch her move her legs while living the dream. Her muffled bark always made him smile. "Where you off to now, girl? What are you after? Don't give up. Go get it!"

She wondered the same of Sam, because on their walks together that summer, she began noticing an increased pace in Sam's gait. Again, she knew something about what was driving Sam. She couldn't quite put her paw on it, but his energy was telling her that he was excited to find more of what he had begun to find.

And now on this day, in another beautiful summer of togetherness and oxytocin, she knew Sam was driving like he had been walking.

Sam knew by Shadow's bark that she was giving him the signal to stop. A few miles later, he turned into a rest stop. She got out quickly, took care of business, and checked a few other messages left by her colleagues. Then did what she always did. Hung very close.

Sam threw her favorite tennis ball, but what was "golden" for Shadow was chasing the ball and chewing it. She wasn't much into the whole "retriever" thing.

Back on the road, the miles passed beneath Charlie RAV4's wheels. Charlie's rearview mirror was doing its thing again, reminding Sam of what he was leaving behind.

He thought of his son, Ben, the jock, who was taking off on his own new journey. He was starting his first year of college on a basketball scholarship, just like his old man. Their relationship, once intentionally better than the one Sam knew with his own father, was now struggling to find its own road since the divorce. Could distance somehow bring them closer? Probably too much to hope for, at least for now. But the hope was coming with him, and Sam appreciated the company.

His daughter, Avery, popped into his mind. She had found her own new life in a group home near her mother. But after a somewhat rocky start, Avery adjusted well to her new community. People with Down syndrome will often do that. Her natural desire to connect, accept, and love built her new life for her. With his plan of making the ninety-minute drive as much as possible, and her mother, Jadyn, living in town, he felt comfortable with the move.

He found good company in his deep gratitude for Avery, knowing that what he had learned from her was riding with him as well.

Another glance at the rearview mirror brought to mind the past summer he had spent with his new friend, Tim. He rehearsed how they first met a year ago at a workshop Tim was leading, in early June. Sam could still hear him talking about living from something that sounded good but wasn't feeling much of at the time—natural Oneness. Natural Oneness with everyone and everything.

At the time it reminded him of Tommy Lang's awesome family when he was growing up. Sometimes after he left the Langs' house, Sam would turn around in their driveway, look back into the house, and wish he could live there. In that love. He knew it was the power of that same longing to live there, in that Oneness of love, that drove him to ask Tim to meet with him again after the workshop.

What followed were the many times he and Tim were together that summer. He saw them at Ole's Tavern. He saw them in the boat. At the playground. Looking up at the stars, and laughing together watching comedy on TV. Staring down at that empty bed at the hospice home, talking about what life and death were all about. "The remembering," as Tim called it. The remembering of love. He saw them back at Ole's Tavern, when Sam needed to tell his new friend what was so difficult to confess.

As he drove, he saw himself in Heather's office in January. Looking out the window and remembering. It was Tim he was with on that day on Fish Lake, when Tim compared the pull of his own soul's delight to the pull he felt from his fishing line.

Sam thought about how Heather's call came at the perfect time. He had spent much of the fall, thinking about his remaining time on earth as Sam Crawford. The mark he wanted to leave on the people he had accompanied.

When he did so, he didn't spend much time thinking about what he wanted to *do*. This new version of Sam Crawford mostly focused on what he wanted to *be*. On the inside. For he had come to realize that it is out of our *being*, that our *doing* arises.

He was indeed growing into becoming more of a human *being*, than a human *doing*. Often stopping and listening for what he already was in the purity of his being. Holding on lightly to the line connecting him with his soul, so he could feel its subtle tugs. Trying to feel how it wanted to lead him into the world of doing.

Shadow didn't always know what Sam was telling her, but being always present in the moment, she could feel Sam's inner world. An inner world that was pulling him down the road to somewhere he seemed to know. She could feel that Sam had learned to trust that pull from within, even when it seemed to make no rational sense. Somehow, it had always been right.

And on this day, she knew it was the same pull they both felt at the rescue when they first saw each other. Her tail now wagging just like it did at their first meeting. Telling her this was another day of new beginnings. It was a classic case of the tail wagging the dog.

Another glance into Charlie RAV4's rearview mirror brought in the students he was leaving behind. He wondered how Will would do in college with his anxiety. How Jamie will handle her dad's death.

He thought again about the incredible potential in Katie. Sometimes when she was particularly amazing in class, he would catch himself thinking, *Dang. She could do anything she wants. I hope she finds out what it could be.*

Sam's heart leapt a bit when he thought of Dante. How would he deal with his parent's divorce? He was so close to his parents.

Will Kerri make varsity this fall as a freshman? *She should. She's that good.*

Would Kelly end up in jail at some point? Sam knew in his heart he had done his best to help her see what only he could. But she listened to other voices. He often worried about her.

When Sam was around her, he often hoped she had a Ms. Bellingham somewhere in her life. "Ms. Bell," his physics teacher, kept Sam grounded his sophomore year of high school, when he was struggling mightily with his father. She grounded him when he was feeling himself close to making bad decisions. He couldn't wait until her class. There was just something about her. For Sam, she was much more than the teacher who lit a fire in him for physics. It was her vibe, her presence, her checking in on Sam when she could see it was needed. *We all need a Ms. Bell,* Sam would often think, when he'd see Kelly walking into class. Carrying her load.

Despite his need for the new. Despite the challenges, the difficult parents, and the family stories some of his students brought with them into class every day, Sam knew he would miss teaching. He would miss the fascination he sometimes saw on his student's faces when they were confronted with how magical and dependable the laws of physics were. He would miss talking with his students before and after class. The checking in. The laughing. The connection.

Could his still-unnamed TV show offer him the same? Now he would be alone, and looking into a sterile TV camera with no face. No story. Gone would be the connection he felt from his students. A companionship he appreciated during the most difficult classes he himself was taking, in what spiritual teachers refer to as this "earth school for the soul."

As for Shadow, she was just fine. School was out, and she was coming off of two glorious summer weeks with Sam: walks, time at the dog park, walks. Chewing and chasing her favorite tennis ball, and rarely retrieving. Walks, hanging out by Sam's feet, and more walks.

As the miles passed beneath her, she had the only thing she needed. Sam. Maybe that was why Sam turned to her for the comfort he so needed. "What am I doing, girl? I have no idea." He felt like he was making another no-look pass behind him again, with the game of his life on the line. *"Who? What will be there this time, girl?"*

Yes. Once again there was a lot riding on Charlie. Charlie RAV4. A lot of baggage, along with the crazy, mixed-up recipe for being human.

Shadow did one of her favorite things, and put her head out the window. She loved feeling the breeze blowing through her. The host of sounds and smells coming in that reminded her of what a gift being a dog really was.

After some time, she settled back down on the back seat, took a deep breath, and offered a long exhale to the world. *Humans,* she thought for the thousandth time, *it seems so hard to be one.*

Good choice, this being a dog, followed another exhale, as she drifted off to her own new adventures. With her legs moving a little, and her muffled bark, they were both on their way. Homeward bound.

FINNEGANS
FOOD & MUSIC & DRINK & SLAINTE

2

Newcastle

NEWCASTLE HAD ITS BEGINNINGS in the flow of the Willoughby River in 1790. One that carried Irish immigrants. Ulster Presbyterians fleeing discrimination and poor harvests.

Those courageous and desperate enough to be the first of their countrymen eventually decided to name the humble town they were building Newcastle. Named after the town many had left, or lived near, in northern Ireland. It is also said these hearty Irish saw in the name "Newcastle" the life or prosperity they were so desperately hoping for.

Word eventually reached their desperate neighbors in northern Ireland. Telling them how they were faring in their new home, and how they viewed its prospects for their countrymen.

Good land here that is opening to settlers. Irish are welcome.
There is a future here, lads, if you so choose. Ad mor ort. (Big luck to ya).

In 1848, a group from the homeland, weary of the potato famine (An Gorta Mór, The Great Hunger), took to heart the words of their neighbors who had ventured before them.

Newcastle. A town that had its beginning in a traditional blessing of their people that dated back to ancient Celtic and pre-Christian times. One given them, and trusted, as they boarded their ship.

May the road rise up to meet you
May the wind be always at your back.

A people knowing only the fear, courage, hope, and despair stubbornly calling them onboard. Trusting a holy breath that had their back, blowing them along an unchartered road rising up to meet them.

Sam Crawford shared their story. Not by ancestry, but by learning to trust the subtle breezes of his intuition. A holy breath blowing him inward. Where he would learn to trust what he was hearing there:

Stop fighting life as it is. Stop fighting yourself.
Turn where the wind is always at your back.
Trust where it wants to lead you.

Sam Crawford knew his risk was laughable, compared to that of the Irish. But he knew he, too, had to trust the signs along the way. Signs telling him the road, the wind, had led him to this exact moment in time. This moment of coming around the bend at the top of a bluff, and seeing one more sign.

Newcastle
Pop. 320,001

Welcome Home

On this day two new immigrants, Sam and Shadow, pulled up to their new home, riding the ship that brought them—the Charlie RAV4. Suffice it to say, "castle" wasn't exactly the first word that popped into his mind.

When Sam accepted the job in January, the station's investors had bought the house as an investment, and were now offering Sam a rent-free place to land, while he and the show hopefully settled in. The home had once stood proudly at the river's edge, where Newcastle began over two hundred years ago.

To look at it, one couldn't help but wonder what stories its brick walls could tell. The sheer size of the house told of how the commerce being carried by the Willoughby River had made some of its early residents quite wealthy. But sitting within Charlie RAV4's point of view, all Sam could see was an old house that looked like something the Addams family would be proud to live in.

Nervously, Sam opened the front door and had his first experience in finding out just how deep the investors' pockets really were. The place had been totally renovated. New wood floors, carpeted areas, furniture, and beautiful decor. A gorgeous, modernized kitchen. A beautiful bedroom that made you question ever getting up in the morning.

An adjacent den, whose built-in mahogany bookshelves, soft carpet, and rock fireplace, made you want to curl up in the safety of its womb, and never be pushed out into the world again. All of this was the work of a talented local interior designer the station had hired.

As Heather had said, the investors were smart with their money, and saw their investment as part of a larger redevelopment of the historic riverfront being planned by the city. "We'll get to the outside of the house soon, Sam," one of the investors would later say. "The inside of anything is most important." Yes it is. For everything from a house to people, to KLUV, where the vision was its heartbeat.

Shadow ran around her new castle with the look of an excited buyer. She slid along the beautiful oak floor, as she tried to stop and check out the next delight.

As the movers arrived and began bringing in a divorced teacher's meager belongings, Shadow ran out the back door and checked the yard for more messages left by those colleagues of hers. After learning that no one had been there for a dog's year, she ran back in, and began looking for what she would declare as "my spot." The place that would be hers, and hers alone. She quickly began circling on a rug by the fireplace. It was during the fifth circling that she determined that all was well. She sat down. Staking her claim.

Her tail, always the truth teller, let the movers know, "Don't worry about me, guys. I'm good right here."

After some hours of unpacking, Sam did what he promised Heather he would do. He called her and she set up a time to get together the next day.

"There's a pub around the corner from the station, on O'Cleary Street, called Finnegan's Pub. Can you be there at noon?"

"Did you say Finnegan's?"

"Yeah. Finnegan's. Why?"

Sam smirked. "Oh, nothing. Just . . . interesting."

"Sol will join us. If you're the first one there, try and get a table in the 'Aisling' room. Welcome home, Sam!"

Sol Weisberg was KLUV's director of programming. Sam had met him back in January during his conversation, a.k.a. interview, with Heather.

On the drive over to Finnegan's the next day, Charlie RAV4 took Sam through a quaint downtown filled with old storefronts. Family-owned small businesses, with their stories of dreams realized and long forgotten. Old-style street lanterns with hanging flowers stood along tree-lined streets, offering the feel of a cozy, small town. The tall bluffs that surrounded the downtown and much of the community gave Newcastle a feeling of safety. Standing strong, they seemed to be declaring to its residents with their quiet strength, "All is well. We've got you!" A feeling that must have felt most welcome to the earliest arrivals, after crossing an ocean of storms and uncertainty.

Finnegan's was the downtown Irish pub that had been a fixture in Newcastle for over one hundred and fifty years. Walk into Finnegan's, and you'll see all that's in a typical Irish pub: dark wood, dark green carpet, a Guinness mirror here, and a Sedgwick's sign there. Folks claiming their Irish heritage (imagined or real). Lifting a pint, and diving into their fish and chips, Irish stew, coddle, or collar and cabbage.

The locals would later tell Sam that if he listened carefully, he could still hear the laughter from tales told a hundred years ago from the old country. Tales increasingly improved over the years. And aye, live Irish music on Friday and Saturday nights, at 8 PM.

Sam arrived early, got their table in the Aisling, took the place in, and felt an alluring kind of welcome. Like coming home to a place he had never been before. A photograph across the way, behind the bar, caught his eye. He walked over and saw it was the pub's founder, Davin Finnegan. Finnegan, who survived growing up in the potato famine, but was still struggling, left the province of Munster in southern Ireland in 1871.

It is said that Munster's ancestors left their descendants the power to endure hardship. The strengths of independence, mutual helpfulness, and discipline. Welcome gifts when building a new business and life in a strange land. All of which would serve the young Finnegan well.

The story goes that when the boat docked that brought Finnegan down the Willoughby to Newcastle, he looked around, decided it reminded him enough of the home he needed to leave, and said, "Beidh se seo ag obair" (This will work). Funny thing about "home" that way. There comes a time when you need to leave it, but you still know it in the desire you have to find it somewhere else. And it was there he lived out the rest of his days, imagining a new castle of his own someday. Finnegan was, as the Irish would say, a "chancer."

Irish lore will tell you that people with the name of Finnegan are often described as kind, compassionate, and intelligent. They are also known for their love of life, and their ability to make people smile.

One look into his eyes, and Sam knew that Davin Finnegan had lived up to his name.

Much like the man whose photo stood proudly at Ole's Tavern in the town he had left. The place Sam first met with Tim. Tom Olsen "founded" Ole's along with his wife, Sue. Ole's didn't have Finnegan's long history. It certainly didn't have its ambience, but it wasn't short on compassion, kindness, and its own quirky way to make people smile.

Looking at the picture behind the bar, Sam turned around to see the community beginning to gather, and began to know what the old Irishman had started so long ago.

That's another funny thing about life. You never know where something wants to go when you give it a start. Things happen that you could never see coming. Sam imagined Davin simply thinking he needed to get out of Munster province, and start a new life with hope, a job, and dependable income. While bringing a touch of the home he wanted to leave.

He, of course, had no idea the friendships that would occur at his up-and-coming pub, much less the marriages and children that would result. He couldn't know of all the "troids," the Irish word for fights, that the marriage of all those pints and men would bring. He couldn't have imagined the laughter, dreams, and heartbreak that these dark walls and green carpet would absorb over the years. Nor how the deaths of people he didn't know existed when he set off from the province of Munster would later grieve him deeply. Forty years of listening to stories will do that to a kind and compassionate heart.

He knew nothing of Cecelia, his wife, that he would meet at a dance some five years later. Their becoming Mr. and Mrs. Davin Finnegan, who themselves would know nothing of Aoife, Erin, Roisin, and Clodagh. Four daughters who would show them joys and sorrows, the depths of which they had never known.

Sam found this to be one of life's most fascinating features—that the reason you *thought* you were doing something would turn out to be only what *got* you to the right place and time. It was there that the heart of the story will be told.

As he pondered this, Sam thought about his new life. His new show. Was it all just a way to get him to where he needed to be?

As with Davin, only the universe seemed to know of the infinite possibilities that could arise out of the choices yet to be made.

And whenever uncertainty occurred for him, thoughts of his buddy Charlie Finnegan usually came to pay him a visit. How he wished Charlie was there. Right now. At Finnegan's Pub. Sitting across from him, giving him grief, and telling him, "I'm right behind you with this KLUV thing, bro!"

Charlie would love this place. And not just the name, Sam thought as he looked around, feeling the tradition. *He'd love the consistency. Dependability.* Yes. Consistency, dependability, have their virtues.

At that, Heather came through the gold-framed door, saw Sam, and joined him in the Aisling room. "Sam! I'm so excited you're here!" This was accompanied by one of her patented wraparound hugs. "This is really starting to happen!"

"This *is* starting to feel real. So, this 'Aisling' room is your favorite?" Sam asked as she sat down.

"Ha! A local told me when I first came, that Davin Finnegan got into this thing where he wanted people to get together in a room that fit their purpose for coming here. People have kind of taken to the tradition here.

"Aisling," she said, looking around the room, "is an Irish girl's name meaning 'dream,' or 'vision.' That's what we're here to discuss, right?" She laughed. "Just playing along, Sam."

"Cool. Tell me about the other names."

"Well, the main space is called 'the Daley.' It means assembly hall. The bigger gatherings and the live music happens there.

"If you're meeting a friend, you might want to get together in 'Cara' over there. Cara means friend. If you need some peace and quiet, the 'Sheehan' is for you," Heather said, pointing to a dark room in the back with gorgeous, inviting, soft lighting. "It means peaceful."

"Beautiful. How about the 'Ardara' over there?

"Isn't that a beautiful name? The Ardara!" she said softly and eloquently, as she closed her eyes. "It means 'fart on a hill.'"

Sam leaned toward her. "Say what?"

Heather tried to keep a straight face, but couldn't. "He just thought it was funny, I guess," she said, laughing as she looked toward the room. "These Americans meeting in a room they thought had such a beautiful story!"

Sam laughed and kept looking over to the Ardara, thinking, *Wonder what kind of occasions call for that room!* He looked back at Heather. "Well, good choice for today."

After ordering their drinks, Heather looked up and saw that Sol had walked in looking like himself. All business. Sol was a nice enough guy, but he always seemed like he needed to be turned a little to the left. You know, "Lefty loosey. Righty tighty."

"So glad you're finally here, Sam. We've got a ton to do, and in programming time, precious little of it to get our ducks in a row."

Heather laughed. "Well, quack, quack! So nice to see you too, Sol."

"Having the usual, Sol?" said the waiter.

"Yeah, yeah."

"Now, Sam. I've been thinking about your show . . ."

Heather looked at Sam with her also patented "Buckle up" look. What followed was a two-and-a-half-hour ride, where Sam again shared the turn his life had taken since last summer, his newfound passions, and personal vision for the show.

As for Sol, well, he kept sharing Sol. Demographics, financials, trends, graphics, charts, projections. Somewhere in there, the following conversation occurred.

"Heather, okay if I have a Guinness while we're working?"

"Only if I join you."

The truth is, the world needs Sols. If only to raise up a toast in gratitude for there being people in this world who love necessary stuff like that.

It all ended with Sol putting a nice corporate bow on it all. "We want the viewer to see themselves in KLUV, and specifically in the vision of the show."

Sam quickly wrote on a paper napkin, and slid it across the table to Sol. "Here's the name of the show."

You Are Love

Sol stared for a long minute at the napkin. "It's a risk, but we'll take it."

Over the next weeks, Sam was indeed still in school. Learning about the world of television: staffing, ideas for format, show topics. The craft of putting a show together: everything from the production team to speaking into the camera. Ideas for introductory music and graphics were bantered about.

The show was scheduled to begin at the end of KLUV's premiere week in September. Sundays from 10 to 11 AM. Sam signed a thirty-show contract that included easing into learning the craft of putting together and presenting feature stories. Beyond that? It was like everything else in television and in life: TBD.

And by the beginning of premiere week, Charlie RAV4 was sporting a new license plate.

U R LUV

You are Love

3

It's Show Time!

"FIVE MINUTES, EVERYONE! FIVE MINUTES," Carly announced to the crew.

Sam sat in his chair on the set. He hadn't been this nervous since he went to the line for two free throws his freshman year, with two seconds left, and his team down by one.

As the makeup artist did her thing, Sam tried to focus on what got him through that night. What got the ball through the net that night. Twice.

Block everything out. You and the teleprompter. You've got this, Crawford. Close the mechanism.

"Close the mechanism" was a line of Kevin Costner's in the movie *For the Love of the Game.* Costner played fictional Detroit Tigers' pitcher Billy Chapel, who first used it standing on the mound at Yankee Stadium, trying to shut off the obnoxious Yankee fans yelling at him.

"Close the mechanism" worked about 90 percent of the time for Sam. A statistic Sol Weisberg would find quite useful.

With the investors pouring money into advertising, and a broad distribution platform of cable, satellite, and online streaming, the research told Sam that he probably had about ninety to one hundred thousand viewers looking at him at that moment. All doing their own research. What is this? Will I like the host and connect with him? Will I watch again?

TV shows and restaurants, he thought. *One bad experience . . . no one's coming back.*

Carly made a fist, flashing her fingers five times. And with her index finger pointing only to Sam, he was on the air. At the line again. Alone.

Sam: Good morning, and welcome to this first airing of *You Are Love*. I'm your host, Sam Crawford. Thank you for joining us. I'd like to spend the first portion of this first show introducing both a little of my story, and what this show, *You Are Love*, is all about.

Sam turns to camera two.

Each week we will feature guest interviews, local musicians and artists, as well as local stories reflecting KLUV's vision, which station manager, Heather Bedford, will be talking about later in the show this morning.

At its heart, *You Are Love* is about authenticity. Sharing with you the human struggle to know what is true and real. What is true and real, or our perception of it, is different for all of us. But is there a truth and reality we *all* share? Is there a common truth of ourselves, and of reality that can guide us forward? Together? That is what we want to lift up on this show.

I want to offer you a bit of *my* "why" and my "what." What brought me here, and why I'm hosting this show. And this is the best way I know. By bringing on my first guest. Shadow, come on, girl!

Shadow runs up to Sam, puts a paw on his leg as Sam rubs her shoulder. Sam motions for her to lie. She lies with her face on Sam's foot, facing the cameras and taking in the strange surroundings.

I want you to meet a beautiful soul and my best friend these days, Shadow. She's a golden retriever. We met at a rescue about two years ago. She was found alone. Left tied to a tree by the side of the road. You can imagine what was going on in her mind.

I was coming off a very painful time in my life. One that was tearing apart the world I had known for a long time. I came to the rescue as Shadow did, feeling lost. Alone. Unsure of my future, or even if there was one. Looking for, well, I wasn't sure. So "rescue" was a good word for our first meeting.

When Shadow and I first saw each other, it was clear to both of us that we'd found in each other what we were looking for. Someone to walk with, as we both take the next steps forward. Sitting on the floor with her that day, we looked at each other and heard each other say, "Let's go home."

Spiritual teacher and author Ram Dass taught, "We're all just walking each other home."

It is the quote that will both shape and end every show. Because that is what we hope you will find here. A home. A space to come and walk together. Taking next steps together toward what we all want in a home—peace, belonging, joy. A space you will feel welcomed as you are. A place to heal, and above all, a place to experience love. A space to walk together and not feel so isolated in these days of so much division.

Perhaps you feel like me living in these times. Lost. Confused. Afraid. Living with the lingering questions of "What is there to hold on to anymore? What is still true and real?"

Maybe you're feeling like Shadow. Abandoned, and bound to something that you want to be free of.

Shadow and I didn't know where we were headed that day as we left the rescue, and you'll be watching a show that will never claim to have all the answers. But hopefully we'll be asking relevant questions. Talking about things that matter, and that are helpful for us all. Listening to our guests and ourselves as we walk together in these unsettling days.

You Are Love does have a spiritual foundation to it. When I use the word "spiritual," it encompasses many things. What gives meaning and purpose to our lives. What gives joy and hope. What carries us through the human experience. By "spiritual" I mean our state of being. What gives us a sense of well-being. What gives life to our life, so to speak.

We do assume a common Source of all that is. An undercurrent of a Source Energy that flows within everyone and everything, enabling us all to live, experience, feel, think, and grow.

Whatever you choose to call the Source, is just that—*your choice*. Whether you identify with the word Source, Energy, the Divine, God, Spirit, Universe, or you identify with any of the names our various religions use. If you don't name it at all, it doesn't matter. We all still *experience* it.

We will gather every Sunday morning at 10 AM, to stand together on that common ground, seeking the way forward.

Hopefully we'll learn from others' experiences and perspectives, as I have from Shadow.

She keeps it simple. On point. Always present. I want to be like her when I grow up. She's what I aspire to be in these confusing times that we have made so complicated.

Sam laughs and looks at Shadow.

Sometimes she looks at me, and I can tell what she's thinking.

You humans! Why do you make it so hard?

As I said, each week's show will feature a guest or two, and also live music from local musicians. We'll feature stories from the larger community of people expressing their own spirit. People seeking to bring about healing, unity, and hope. And in doing so, raising it up within themselves and us.

Shadow will often be with us. Reminding us. Helping us remember. Right, girl?

Shadow stands and puts her head on Sam's lap.

With that, we'll be back with my second guest, after this short break.

Carly: *And we're off.*

Commercial Break

During the break, Sam hears Sol in his earpiece. "Good start, Sam."

Tim is seated, and they review their plan.

Carly: *Five, four, three . . .*

Sam: Welcome back. I want to introduce you to my second guest.

Tim's name appears on screen.

I met Tim last summer when, as I said, I was lost. Trying to figure out what was next. I was out for a walk, and saw a poster about a workshop titled "Natural Oneness," led by my guest. Oneness wasn't something I was feeling at the time. Tim, you've become a dear friend, and I thank you for being with us this morning.

Tim: Oh, Sam. Thanks for having me. I cherish our friendship.

Sam: This friendship evolved after the workshop and over the course of several times together last summer. You invited me to meet you at a variety of places. Settings intentionally chosen to help me "remember," was the word you kept using. The first was at Ole's Tavern.

Tim: You didn't see that comin', did you! So many great conversations happen in a tavern!

We had amazing discussions while we were fishing, in nature, listening to music, finding that spark of creativity, sitting under the stars, playing a round of golf, watching comedy on TV. We even met at a hospice home, standing next to an empty bed, talking about life-and-death issues.

I believe the experiences we all have are here to help us remember. Remember what is true. To help us remember our *deepest* truth. That's just how I see experiences. We all have our own ways of seeing things.

The Heart of the Conversation

Tim: What did Shadow help you remember, Sam?

Sam: That connection, belonging, and caring are my oxygen. I had known that in my life before, and was lost without it. When I knew it again, I felt like I was returning home.

Tim: A home you both made for each other. Which is why I think what's going on today in our country—all the division, anger, and fear, feels so "off." So exhausting.

Sam: Like something is just, fundamentally wrong. It just drains the life right out of you.

Tim: Exactly. Let me ask you, what is the *greatest* thing Shadow has shown you?

Sam and Shadow look at each other…

Sam: That's easy. Love. And unconditional love, at that. No matter how I am, I only feel love from her. I'd like our viewers to see what inspired the name of this show. Tim, would you roll up your sleeve, so our viewers can see your tattoo?

Tim rolls up his sleeve, and the camera zooms in on his right forearm.

Sam: Can you all see it? It reads, *you are love*. What's the story?

Tim: This actually came to be as a result of my paying attention. Paying attention to when I knew a lasting contentment. A deep joy. Similar to your experience with Shadow.

It was always when I knew love, in one form or another. To when I was either loving, or being loved. When I was simply kind. So I began to realize, remember what I am, what *we* all are, at our core. Love!

[Tim laughs.] I imagine it wrinkled up twenty years from now, saying "yr r lv!"

Sam: Ha! Well, time is relentless. You shared a painting with me that attempts to visualize the heart of what we talked about last summer.

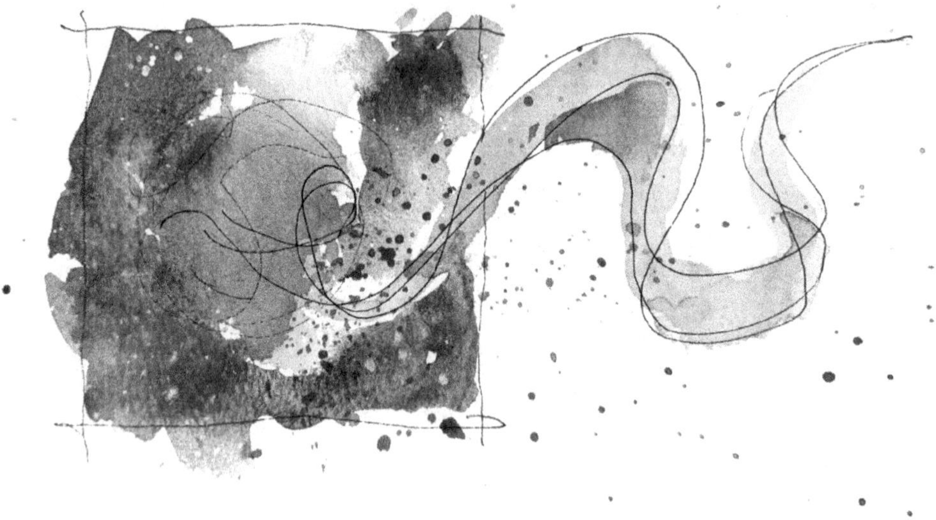

Tim: This was painted for me by my friend, Bill. It attempts to show an energy that is the Source of everything. And everything that emerges from it—you, me, your viewers, all that is around us and within us, *is* that energy in its essence.

And it makes sense to me, that the essence of this energy is a profound love, given everything we know of what makes us feel truly alive. What makes life work, which is this profound, life-giving love.

Sam: Interesting. As I said before, we can call this anything we want, or not label it at all. It doesn't matter. We all share the same truth in the experience.

Tim: That is what connects us all. What connects everything. And I think most of us who have some years under our belt have observed that we're all basically seeking the same thing.

And it makes sense, at least to me, that we're seeking the same thing, because we all *came* from the same thing. We all *are* the same thing in our essence—love.

Sam: And in that we will walk together, week to week through this show. Sharing experience.

Learning. Listening. Listening to our guests and ourselves. Listening to each other. We hope this show inspires conversation with your friends, as we encourage each other to stay on the journey.

Tim, can't thank you enough for this time together. We'll be right back, with KLUV's station manager, Heather Bedford, who will share with you the vision of KLUV.

Carly: *And we're off.*

Commercial Break

Carly: *Five, four, three . . .*

Heather: Good morning. I'm Heather Bedford, KLUV's station manager. I would like to share with you the "why" of KLUV. Our mission is to lift up the human spirit, which has been this week's focus and will continue to be.

Video of various stories play silently as Heather speaks.

We will offer you stories of love and hope. Stories like this group of women who gather weekly at the Newcastle Community Center, to knit hats for babies in the NICU at Newcastle hospital.

Another story about Palestinian and Israeli women who come together weekly to support one another. They've found their common humanity in their mutual grief over losing a son or daughter.

This story of the local Better Angels chapter, where people from both sides of the political spectrum come together to do the difficult work of learning to listen and talk with one another, in an atmosphere of respect.

Another story about the community coming together to raise money for medical bills accrued by a Newcastle resident, who was struck by a distracted driver.

And this related story of people gathering to honor and remember a transgender man who was brutally beaten here in downtown Newcastle just last week.

These are stories of our community lifting up the human spirit. This is what KLUV is all about. We hope our programming inspires us all to go out into the world around us, lifting up what we all have in common, and are at our core. Love. So, it is our privilege to offer *You Are Love* every Sunday morning. We'll be right back.

The end of the show

Sam: Thank you for sharing your time with us this morning. Next week my guest will be Dr. Constance Delauria, professor of Holistic Health at Newcastle University.

As mentioned earlier, Ram Dass taught, "We're all just walking each other home." I hope you'll join me each week as we walk each other home.

Shadow pops up at the word "walk."

[Sam laughs.] Looks like it's time for us to walk each other home! You are love.

Carly: *And we're off.*

After the show, Sam told Tim he'd love to take him to his new tavern. "It's an Irish pub called Finnegan's. I think you'll love it. The owner, Kelly, knows Shadow. She lets her sit with me at a back table. Actually, a lot of folks know Shadow by now. I'm starting to think she could run for mayor."

When they walked in, Sam introduced Tim to Kelly and to a few other folks. They felt everything they spoke of on the show.

After lunch, Tim left, and Sam and Shadow walked home. Sam was busy thinking about the show. Shadow, meanwhile, had her paws on the ground. Feeling the joy of being. With Sam.

4

What He Didn't Say

AS NIGHT SETTLED IN, SAM COULDN'T. He was feeling something he'd known forever, it seemed. An adrenaline that wouldn't shut down. Something he had known before big games.

He looked at Shadow sleeping on the floor next to him. With her soft whimpers and legs moving, she told him of yet another adventure. "Looks like we're both busy, girl."

He got up, went down to the den, and started a fire. As the rocks from the Willoughby's edge warmed, he continued replaying the show in his cluttered head. A spark exploded, igniting thoughts of everything in his story that he *hadn't* told his viewers that morning.

He gazed at the five sections of built-in bookshelves, crafted so long ago. They gave off a look of stability that he needed that night, as he began to imagine them holding a library of his life.

He thought of the man he had wanted everyone to see that morning on his show. How we are all selective storytellers, while knowing a thousand others that will never be told. After all, what if they knew?

"Will you love *this* person? No? How about *this* one?"

He imagined the section closest to the door holding books telling of his childhood.

Books describing his relationship with his sister, Karen, a year older. They were close, especially when they were young. They pretty much had to be. Their father's wounds would pay them a regular visit, courtesy of Frank Crawford's best friend and betrayer, "Jack," as his father often called him—referring to Jack Daniel's whiskey.

Frank, Sam, and Karen had two primary ways of relating to each other. The first was in a mutual unmet desire to connect. For Karen and Sam, it was known in a desire for what their friends knew. A simple hug. Time shared cuddled next to him, reading a book. A tuck in at night from him.

For Frank, it was known in an occasional attempt to connect. But the awkwardness only served to show all three that he was currently unavailable.

The second revealed itself when Frank would either come home drunk, or would take care of the task at home. It was then that he often added anger to the toxic recipe that he served to his family.

One particular time forever shaped the future of Sam and Karen's relationship with their father. Sam was five, and Karen was six, when their mother made a quick visit to their next-door neighbor's house to return something. Frank came home at least five sheets to the wind. One look at him, and the two did what they always did. They ran upstairs to their rooms, shut the door, and escaped into worlds they had created for a time such as this.

Frank came stumbling up the stairs. Doors were locked, so Frank banged first on Sam's door. "What the hell, Sam?" Then on Karen's door. "Open the damn door!" Sam ran out into the hallway. "Daddy! Stop!" With that, Karen opened her door and saw her dad turn and push Sam away, causing him to slam hard against the wall. "Don't talk to your father like that!" He stormed out, stumbled straight down the stairs, and out the front door.

Sam and Karen watched the window as he stumbled down the snow-covered street and around the corner. He didn't return until his children, too afraid to tell their mother, had fallen asleep to this horrible story.

Frank left more than the house. From that day on, as far as Karen and Sam were concerned, their father abandoned any hope of them ever feeling safe and loved around him. The two things any child desperately wants from their father.

Instead they watched their father stumble away, doing what they always did. Holding each other as they cried. They would keep holding each other until they both realized they found in each other what they were seeking in that crazy man stumbling down the street.

And of course they kept doing what children often do in such a story. They thought this was all their fault. And so began an endless search for what it was they needed to *stop* doing, and for what they needed to *do* to make it all better. To make *him* better. Maybe then.

They sent out their endless "*Do you love me now?*"—excelling in their studies and in their sports. But it was never enough. Instead, Frank Crawford held court at Oscar's Bar, searching for his "enough" at a bottle's bottom. Leaving deep wounds that could only heal to scars on their tender, vulnerable hearts.

It wasn't *all* bad that he wasn't at their games. Eventually Sam noticed a curious thing. His coach, Coach Ferguson, often spoke to his players about the importance of breathing properly. "The average person breathes about twenty to twenty-five thousand times a day," he'd say. "It will serve you and the team well to learn to do it right."

What was curious to Sam was that even after many frenzied trips up and down the court, he was still breathing easier than he ever did around his dad. Sam would learn to know the "rightness" of a lot of things by how he was breathing within it. "Deep. Unforced. Lateral," as Coach would say.

As for their mother, Betsy, she was a lovely woman, with a fierce love for her children. It was after Sam left home and went to college that he came upon the "Tale of the Two Wolves."

It was the reading of this short tale of unknown origin that helped him understand his mom.

Tale of the Two Wolves

One evening an old Cherokee told his grandson about a battle that goes on inside people. He said, "My son, the battle is between two 'wolves' inside us all.

"One is Evil. It is anger, envy, jealousy, doubt, sorrow, regret, greed, arrogance, self-pity, guilt, resentment, inferiority, lies, false pride, superiority, and ego.

"The other is Good. It is joy, peace, love, hope, serenity, humility, kindness, benevolence, empathy, generosity, forgiveness, truth, compassion, and faith."

The grandson thought about it for a minute and then asked his grandfather,

"Which wolf wins?"

The old Cherokee simply replied,

"The one you feed."

Betsy Crawford could always feel the Evil wolf lurking. Circling. Waiting…waiting to pounce at any sign of weakness. To feed on Betsy's self-doubt and inferiority. To feast on its favorite: her self-loathing. Thriving on Frank's verbal abuses, and a beaten-down Betsy Crawford believing them:

Why'd you do that? What the hell is the matter with you? Can't you do anything right?

You'd be nothing without me!

She tried to escape by seeking a life outside of it all. A space that was safe and free. She found a job at a nearby card shop, and loved the camaraderie of the staff, and the pleasant exchanges with the customers. Her Good wolf was seen by everyone there, except her, in her kindness and compassion. When she'd make the smallest of mistakes, it would show up for only her to see.

What's the matter with you? Can't you do anything right?

But there was one place in her life where her Good wolf roamed free. One sacred space where she could catch a glimpse of it. It was when she was with her cubs. She'd often wrap one arm around Sam, the other around Karen, and hold on for dear life. There they were, listening to the Good wolf saying,

I'm here for you. I love you. You are enough. We are enough.

Around such sacred space, Betsy built an impenetrable wall. When Frank's Evil wolf paid a visit to their shared space, she refused it access. It was there the Good wolf was fed.

So the question and the answer remained the same for her as it is in everyone's tale. Which wolf will thrive? The one you feed.

He imagined the second bookshelf holding the stories of his college days.

They would describe his leaving for college, feeling "homeward bound." A home he could build for himself. One filled with friends and possibilities. Consistency and dependability.

When he arrived, he quickly found it in his basketball family. He immediately connected with the coaches and players on his recruiting visit. He lived with five teammates in a house just off campus. The book would tell of his finding the home he longed for in his extremely structured day: class, tutors, practice, study. Game days were class, game. Repeat.

He quickly became close to a point guard on the team. He was no Charlie. Sam knew what Charlie was going to do. Booker, on the other hand, was an incredibly creative and spontaneous point guard. Driving with the ball and making passes that no one could see coming, including Booker.

Booker was a fun-loving, "chill" kind of guy. When he stepped on the court he didn't change. He worked hard, but he almost always played with a smile on his face. Sam had never seen anyone play like that. By the look of Booker's face, it was *always* going well.

When Sam asked Booker about his smile, Booker said that he played better when he smiled. "High school coach told us, 'You do *anything* better with a smile on your face.'" Booker would tell him, "You relax. You expect good things and they come to you. The stuff that doesn't work out doesn't bother you as much, and you have more fun. So why not?"

Sam thought about that for weeks. You think about and explore a lot of things in college. That's what you're there for. When Sam finally tried it, he found Booker's wisdom to ring true.

In a philosophy class his sophomore year, Sam started to wax philosophically about the difference eleven inches of height had made in his life. Next to a man of average height, 5'9", Sam Crawford towered eleven inches over him. His 6'8", 230-pound frame naturally giving him what we all want—to be seen. People often spoke of his height. It was usually the first thing they noticed about him.

As a result, people treated him differently. For some reason, people seemed to respect him more. Add being a successful athlete, and they treated him as if he was something special. Being young, it was hard for him not to buy into it at times. It seemed odd to him though. After all, it wasn't exactly a personal accomplishment. But he often found himself thinking, "*If that's the way it is, I guess I'll take it.*"

As Sam sat staring at the bookshelf, his mind went back to an evening under the stars with his friend Tim. He recalled their conversation about how incredibly small they felt in the vastness of the universe. They spoke of the billions of light years it would take for light to reach the end of the universe, and how there really couldn't be an end in an ever-expanding universe. All he could think was *Compared to the universe, my six feet eight inches is laughable!*

He looked back on what his laughable height had given him, and shook his head. A full scholarship. A new life and home in college. People cheering for him. Playing in a Division I program on TV. An identity and sense of worth. *Those eleven inches gave me Booker,* he thought. *I would've never met Heather. Without her I wouldn't be sitting here.*

As his eyes moved down a shelf, he imagined its books telling the story of how his height had brought him his future wife. In the seats at Sam's games his freshman year sat another freshman, Jadyn Calloway. Jadyn was an athlete herself in high school. Her sport was volleyball. She knew herself what a few inches had given her. At 6'2", with a huge vertical jump, she had set a state record for "kills" and blocked shots. It earned her a scholarship.

But at just her second practice, she jumped at the net to do what she does best. What she'd done thousands of times. But this time her knee crumpled. She felt the pop. Heard the thought, *This is bad,* as she went down. She rolled on the court in pain, looking up at the stars popping up in her own night sky.

While rehabbing after an ACL surgery, she went to a men's basketball game. She found herself keeping her eye on one player. She saw herself in how "Crawford" positioned himself before he went up for a rebound, or to block a shot. She noticed how well he moved on the court for a big man. Something she herself took pride in.

So when they were in a second semester class together their sophomore year, she took one more leap, and asked Sam if he'd like to go for a walk near campus.

The Walk

He noticed it right away in his breathing. Deep, like he couldn't take in enough of her. Not forced. It all seemed so easy with her that day. In his breath, he could hear Coach Jenkins telling him, *Pay attention. She's the one!*

He had a lot of time to notice because Jadyn did most of the talking. It wasn't that she didn't want to learn about him. She was simply touched by the questions he kept asking her. His way of asking and listening, telling her he really wanted to know. Her. *All* about her.

He wanted to know what was funny to her. What her family was like. Where she found joy. What annoyed her. What was important and not important to her. What her favorite "whatever" was. And in all of that, she began to know Sam. The part of him she cared most about. His heart.

Sam loved the strong and determined way Jadyn went about everything in her life. How consistent and dependable she was. And he loved her tenderness when he spoke of his struggles with his father. He loved the feel of her soothing eyes penetrating his wounded heart.

He welcomed how easy it was to share the stress and pressure he was feeling playing in a big-time basketball program. The expectations. He surprised himself when he told her how exhausted he was sometimes, always trying to look strong and confident.

Jadyn loved Sam's vulnerability that night. His gentle and kind heart. His patient listening, and deep respect for her. His laugh that was as big as he was.

In the next couple of months, Sam realized he was finding the lighthouse he had been seeking. That immovable light that would guide him to the safe harbor he longed for.

The next three years gave both of them time to see other sides of what they loved the most on their first walk. Jadyn saw how Sam's vulnerability left wounds that sometimes showed themselves in sudden outbursts of anger, revealing just how deep those scars were on his gentle and tender heart. She began to see how his deep listening and respect for her came from not having received the same from his father.

Sam would see how Jadyn's strong, determined confidence came out twisted in an annoying stubbornness. One that was fed by a deep-seated frustration with men not taking the women in her family seriously. Something she had zero tolerance for.

In those three years they learned to adapt, accept, and eventually decide that they were imperfectly perfect for each other. And in their senior year, Sam Crawford found himself on his healthy knee, where they had their first walk. "Jadyn, you're my home. Will you marry me?"

My height gave me all that? Go figure.

A gaze at the third section of the bookshelf prompted him to see a book from college leaning up against the frame: *The Complete Works of William Shakespeare.*

He thought of his favorite Shakespeare quote, "All the world's a stage, and all the men and women merely players."

Characters. That's what we all are, Sam reminded himself, *in a giant play.*

Just for fun, he took a theatre arts class in college, where he learned how actors need to totally commit to their character. They lose themselves and "become" the character. If successful, both they and the audience are changed and become something else, at least for a time.

Jadyn and I were good actors in college, he thought, as he remembered Jadyn playing the "nothing's going to stop me" athlete in recovery, and on the volleyball court. He was the "leave it all on the court" basketball star. *We were totally committed.*

With a nod to his high school teacher "Ms. Bell," Sam decided to major in physics his freshman year. Jadyn, as a result of seeing the new life rehab had given her, changed her major to sports medicine.

And after a graduation and wedding ceremony, they moved their "play" to another town, Brayden, with Jadyn cast as a therapist at Williams Sports Medicine Center. She began working with the high school girls' volleyball team as an assistant. The "audience" saw her as a coach, wife, friend, neighbor, and active community member.

The first day Sam walked onto the stage as the new physics teacher, he drew the same reaction from his "audience" that he always did. "Whoa!" Again, Sam thought what he always thought. *I'll take it if it helps.*

Sam began working occasional weekends with a sports program for kids with special needs. He even tried out for a part in the Big Brothers program. The script there calling for him to devote time to his little brother, Justin. Sam loved the role. Their chemistry coming from their not having much of a father in their lives.

Justin was totally into sports, and Sam would often take him to an outdoor basketball court, showing his "little brother" some fundamentals. He took Justin to games, followed by the proverbial chocolate ice cream. Justin ate it up.

So *The Sam and Jadyn Show* had opened, but it seemed easier when first written. Fewer characters. Less complicated, demanding, and exhausting. *They* were the arc of the storyline. Now there was so much pulling them away from the original script. Away from each other. The tricky part was the stories were written with good intentions, and the characters all so alluring.

With them increasingly on opposite sides of the stage, yet another character entered center stage. Their son, Ben, was welcomed with open and loving arms, to be sure. But now the decision needed to be made on what needed to exit. The hardest one for Sam was what to do with Justin. Justin needed him, and Sam couldn't just walk offstage.

Three years later another new character joined them at center stage. A daughter, Avery, with Down syndrome. Where was the story going now? The day's scenes ending as they always did, with Sam and Jadyn meeting back at center stage and falling into bed exhausted, with the curtain closing on that day's performance.

And then the lights went out. Or so it seemed. A new show, *Covid-19*, opened in March of 2020. They suddenly found themselves in an entirely new play. One that was dark and fear-filled, leaving them feeling isolated. With everyone feeling like an audience member, the characters talked to each other on screens in this virtual play. Sam had to learn to teach and perform on screen. Students who desperately needed to share a stage with live actors now felt isolated in their one-person shows from home.

Isolation is sometimes not the best place to act from, and it was from there that Sam began looking for someone with whom he could share a common storyline. Stage right, he began FaceTiming and later meeting with a teacher friend, stage left. The problem was, she wasn't a he and there was a big red line at center stage that should never be crossed . . . but it was.

What eventually followed was a scene of Jadyn crying and screaming, "Fuck, Sam! What the hell! How could you? To me? To Ben and Avery? To us?"

How could I? A question that Sam would ask himself a thousand times. A question with no answer. At least not one that could stand up under a spotlight.

Fast forward to Sam now sitting alone in an empty apartment. Scared as hell.

As Sam's eyes moved over to the fourth section, he imagined books filled with stories of where his life was a year ago.

One with a chapter describing a conversation with a friend. "Sometimes I guess you have to let yourself be down," he told her.

"Fall as far as you'll go. Then one day you realize you're tired of it down there. You realize the 'down' is flushed out of you. You finally look up and know that you *can* get up. But then what?"

The next chapter telling the story of Sam later looking out his bedroom window and seeing a little girl learning how to ride her bike without training wheels. She struggles as the bike slowly wobbles to the left and right. Her father a little behind her, encouraging her to pedal a little faster and it would get easier. And so it was. "Yes! You're doing it! Just keep going, sweetheart!"

Just step. Just peddle. Get in motion and see where it takes you, the big guy would tell himself. So, he gets up, takes a walk, not having a clue where he was going, and his eyes settle on a poster for a workshop.

His whole life had served as training wheels up to that point. Now it was about learning to trust that inner voice telling him, "Go." "Don't." "Do it." "Don't." "Keep moving forward. You've got this."

The fifth section's emptiness told of a life yet to be published. Empty. Except for one small book which began telling the tale of the day when "the new guy" walked into a TV station, and . . .

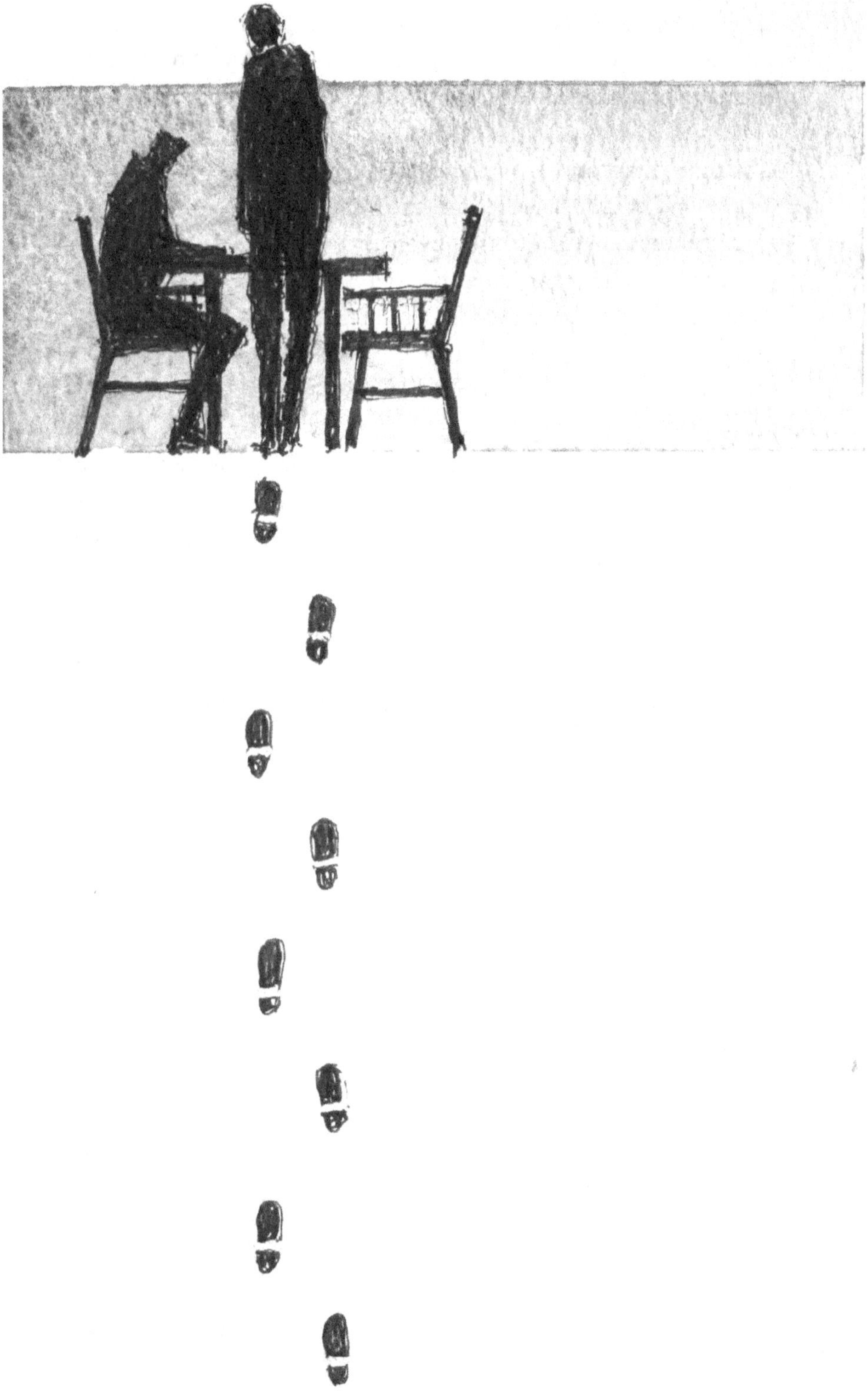

5

The Ninth Step

AND THERE IT WAS. After a night of revisiting his story, it came to visit *him* the very next day. In the form of a most surprising and unwelcome note waiting for him on his desk at KLUV the following morning.

Your father called. He said it's urgent.

In between calls, meetings, emails, and more calls, Sam spent most of the day looking at the note. Picking up his phone and putting it down. Picking it up. Putting it down. The word "urgent" kept staring up at him. Finally at 4 PM, Sam Crawford did what he hadn't done for three years. He talked to Frank Crawford.

"Oh, thank God! Thanks for calling me, Sam. Sorry about calling it urgent, but I thought it'd be the only way you'd call back. Well, actually it *is* urgent, at least for me. I've joined a new AA group. I'm on my ninth step. You and Karen are the first on my list of people I need to admit my wrongs to. Would you be willing to meet with me? I'd appreciate it more than you know."

An uncomfortable pause ended with Sam exhaling and saying, "Well, you've never gotten to the ninth step before. I'll give you that."

With his eyes closed, and a wince on his face telling him he was going to regret it, Sam Crawford said to the man he only shared a name with, "Okay. When?"

"Any way it could happen this week, Sam?"

"Whoa. You're not kidding around. Where you living? Could you come to Newcastle?"

"Sure. I'm a couple of hours away."

Sam hesitated when he started suggesting Finnegan's. *Inviting an alcoholic to a pub? Maybe not your best idea, Crawford.* His father said he could handle it. They set it up for Friday.

Sam was nervous and uncertain all week, and he had good reason to be. Sam and his father had something in common that they had shared forever, it seemed. They both would look at each other and often wish they hadn't.

Sam's problem was he saw in his father the person he feared he *could* be. Being around alcohol always made him nervous. Their looking so much alike didn't help either.

Frank's problem was he saw in Sam the person he *wanted* to be, but knew he wasn't. Sam was focused, determined, kind, able to connect with people. Someone folks looked up to in more ways than one.

All that came flooding back when Frank Crawford walked through Finnegan's front door with the gold trim around it. There he was. All 6'6" of him. Sam once again saw the stride they shared. He always resented it. In fact, when Sam was around ten, he actually tried to walk differently than his dad. But it just took too much effort. It's hard when your body naturally wants to do something, and your pain is pushing you to do something else. Anything else. DNA can be a bitch sometimes.

A lot can happen in a distant father's forty-foot walk to his forty-two-year-old son. In those forty feet, each step walked him back to that five-year-old boy. The disappointment that was still breaking his heart. The hurt and anger. The flashback so clear in his mind of that day when Frank Crawford pounded on Karen's door. He was right back in her bedroom where he and Karen watched their dad stumble down the street from her window. He saw himself looking up from the court, yet again, and seeing only his mother in the bleachers. Thankful to see her, but with the same thoughts in his head. *Really? Again?*

However, this time Frank Crawford *did* show up. And this time they were both in the game. Two Crawfords suddenly sitting across from each other, looking each other in the eye for the first time in three years. Davin Finnegan could have never imagined it.

"Sorry. Gonna need a moment here," Sam said as he looked around the Sheehan (peace) room they were sitting in. He was hoping to invoke its magic. Finding none, he took a deep breath. His exhale telling him, *Okay, this is happening.*

"Sam, when I heard about KLUV through a friend at AA, I knew I needed it. So, I watched *You Are Love* for the first time on Sunday morning, and holy crap! There you were! I had to walk up close to the screen. I couldn't believe it was you! That's how I knew you were here."

"Yeah, I figured that might be how. Um, how are you?"

"I'm okay."

In the proverbial awkward silence that followed, Sam thought, *Three years? Hell, a lifetime! And that's all we've got?* At this point Sam was starting to feel like he actually had found that occasion appropriate for the Ardara (fart) room.

"You said you're going to an AA group?"

"Yeah. Nine months now. I was at a new bottom. I just decided, 'To hell with it. To hell with trying on my own. To hell with the lying.' I knew my bottoms before, but this time I felt like I had totally played my hand. No cards left to BS my way through. I was done.

"I heard about this meeting. They call themselves 'The Power of Collective Powerlessness.' I don't know. Something pulled me there. Maybe it was the word 'powerless.' It was all I knew. So I went, and I loved it. There's something counterintuitive about it, but a room full of people who feel powerless is a very powerful thing. I don't know. I can't explain it. I don't know how it works. I just know it does. I've met some great drunks there. Good dudes. My sponsor is awesome. Has a terrific crap detector."

"Alright. I'm happy for you. I hope it helps."

An outburst of laughter from the adjacent Aisling room broke the tension for a few moments, but five-year-old Sam quickly found himself trying to move the conversation along.

"You mentioned you're on your ninth step. You said you wanted to share it with me?"

"Yeah, sure. I don't want to keep you. I'm sure you're busy." Frank nervously got out his handwritten notepad paper that looked like it had been folded and opened more times than he had taken a drink. He carefully unfolded it, flattened it out, took a deep breath, and closed his eyes.

"Oh shit! This is hard. Even harder than it was writing it. Okay, here goes . . ."

> *Sam, I know that I hurt you, and disappointed you more times than either of us can count. I need you to hear that I am so, so sorry.*

With that, tears welled up in Frank Crawford's eyes. Something Sam had never seen from him. Ever. As they built up, and the first one fell down his left cheek and landed on the paper like a long-awaited arrival, Frank gave himself a moment.

> *I know I provided for you, Karen, and your mother as best I could. But beyond that, I was a horrible father. I wasn't there for you.*
>
> *From my time at meetings, it's finally gotten through to me that I wasn't there for you because I was never there for myself. I should have told you that I love you. But I never did because I didn't love myself.*
>
> *I hated myself, Sam. I always have. I know I didn't look like it, but I saw what I was doing. I saw what I was, and I despised myself. Maybe as much as you despised me. Then I drank to try and cover it all up, which made everything happen all over again.*
>
> *I saw the look of sadness, disappointment, embarrassment. The hurt in your eyes when you looked at me.*
>
> *Please don't think I'm trying to make excuses. I'm not. No more excuses. No more bullshit. I'm finally trying to own up to what I've done. Be accountable for once in my life.*
>
> *Sam, I'm sorry I wasn't at your games like I should have been. I need you to know that I wanted to be, more than I can say. But I actually thought you'd be better off without me there. In fact, there were many days I thought you'd all be better off without me around at all.*

I abused your mother. I don't recall ever hitting her. Maybe I did when I was really drunk. God, I hope I didn't. She never said anything about that happening. At least that I can remember.

But I sure as hell know that I abused her in how I treated her. How I talked to her. How I wasn't there for her either.

I'm starting to see now that I dumped all my pain on her, you, and Karen. I know you were a much better brother to her than I was a father. Thank you from the bottom of my heart.

I know I can't undo what I've done. I can't get back those years that we could have had.

I know I deserve nothing from you. Your being willing to hear me out now is more than I deserve.

I want you to know that I was always so proud of you. I was in awe of what I heard you did on the court. But I most admired the person you are in spite of me. I thank your mother for how she raised you and Karen.

I often visit her at her grave. I tell her how thankful I am. I tell her lots of things I wished I had said when she was here. I hope she can hear me.

Please know, Sam, there were so many times I looked at you and saw the person I wanted to be.

I am really trying to love myself. And more than anything in this world, I would like for us to have a relationship of some kind. I would love it if you could find it in your heart to forgive me. But I understand if neither of those are possible.

And with that, Franklin Lyle Crawford looked up from his worn-out paper, looked through his tired eyes into Sam's, and said the three words Sam had spent his whole life waiting to hear. "I love you, Sam."

Hard to tell how long the silence was. How long Sam looked around that room. How long Sam looked anywhere, except at the man who just took his ninth step toward his son.

"I'm sorry. I need a minute," Sam muttered. He walked quickly into the men's room, and plunked himself down in the nearest stall. Perhaps someone heard the fist pounding. He didn't care. The walls surrounding him, and the porcelain pew provided the sanctuary he needed. Yes, there are sacred spaces in this world that often go overlooked.

"Where the *hell* has that been all my life?" he yelled.

Then it was like he was listening to two people yelling at him. The first voice, the one that had been walking with him his whole life, yelled, *Go out there and tell that son of a bitch to get back in his car and get the hell out of your life!* The other voice, one totally unfamiliar and sympathetic to his father said, *Your own father just made himself vulnerable as hell, and that's all you've got? What's wrong with you, Crawford?* The familiar voice countered, *You know what he did to you! You've got every right to be angry and pissed as hell!*

But you saw his face, said the strange, new voice. *He's really trying this time.* The other voice added, *Look at you! You think of yourself as all spiritual now? On this great path? Ha! You're a joke!*

Then a calm and confident third voice that seemed to be patiently waiting its turn calmly said, *This IS the path,* as if it were simply a matter of fact.

Back and forth it went until they seemed to have said their piece. In the clarity of the increasing silence, Sam could hear the calm voice telling him he needed time, and that he needed to be careful with his words. He suddenly knew he could blow this onetime chance with whoever the guy was sitting across the table. *Alright . . . I can do this!*

He walked back to the table, sat down, and said something he had long ago given up imagining he'd ever say. "I know what you just did . . . was hard as hell for you. I respect that, and I'm happy you're doing the work you're doing for yourself. But I'm going to need some time to be with this. I hope you understand."

Frank couldn't hide his disappointment as he stared down at the table. Finally nodding his head. "Sure, Sam. I understand. Yeah. Take your time."

As the man who looked and walked so annoyingly like him was getting into his car, Sam leaned down toward the half-opened driver's side window, not having a clue what to say next.

"Thanks . . . son, for listening. It means the world to me."

With that, Frank Crawford drove off. As he stood watching, Sam realized he had no idea where he was going. He hadn't asked him where he was living. He did notice how strange the word "son" felt, and how he knew the word "dad" wasn't anywhere within him.

Sam walked back to his office staring only at the sidewalk. Sitting down at his desk, he looked again at the note. *Urgent* was all he saw.

community
Connection
LOVE
Kindness

6

You Are Love

Your Body. Your Truth Teller.

"FIVE MINUTES EVERYONE," CARLY SHOUTED as Sam took his seat on the set. Shadow, who already knew where her spot was, laid down next to Sam's foot.

Carly: *And five, four, three . . .*

Sam: Good morning, everyone, and welcome back to this second edition of *You Are Love*. It's our hope that this show helps you remember that you are KLUV's vision of "Lifting Up the Human Spirit," and that your deepest truth is love.

I'm your host, Sam Crawford. And if you didn't see our first show last Sunday, this is Shadow. A golden retriever, dear soul, and best friend. She'll be with us from time to time.

Our guest today is someone many of you know. Constance Delauria is a professor of holistic health at Newcastle University. She writes a popular syndicated column, Life's Labyrinth, and is a frequent guest on podcasts, radio, and television. Welcome, Constance.

Constance: Thanks for having me, Sam. I'm very excited not only to be here, but excited about the vision of KLUV. It is so needed. And hello, dear Shadow.

Shadow gets up and takes a couple of steps toward Constance. She sniffs, sits, and looks up to Sam. "She checks out. You can continue."

Sam: Constance, we invited you, and are inviting you, the viewers, to focus on "community" this morning. What it means, how vital it is to our well-being, and what the need for community says about our deepest truths.

Constance, as a professor of holistic health, why is community so vital to our well-being?

Constance: We are created for connection. Science, specifically neuroscience, confirms that humans are clearly hardwired for connection. Our brains are biologically designed to seek and form relationships with others. This is supported by the presence of mirror neurons that help us understand and empathize with other people's emotions and actions. From an evolutionary perspective, social connection was crucial for survival in early human societies.

That's strictly the science part of the answer, but I think for all of us, there are some deeper, spiritual questions and answers that are more meaningful.

Sam: Tell us more.

The Heart of the Conversation

Constance: Why? Why are we designed in this way? I watched your show last week when your guest talked about the fundamental truth of reality being a Oneness in Love. That core truth reveals itself in our very biology. Our bodies and minds are constantly reminding us that we are love.

Sam: How so?

Constance: You mentioned kindness last Sunday. The physical benefits of kindness are enormous:

Kindness increases serotonin, dopamine, which improve your mood, and just plain makes you feel good. Kindness reduces anxiety and depression.

Kindness improves your heart health by causing it to produce oxytocin.

Sam: *[Laughing]* Ah yes, the "love hormone." *[Sam looks at Shadow.]* I'd like to introduce you to my oxytocin dealer.

Constance: Yes! Everyone out there who has a beloved pet. Thank them every day for being your supplier!

Kindness also reduces pain by releasing endorphins, which are the body's natural painkillers. Kindness makes you stronger and more energetic. People who volunteer tend to have fewer aches and pains. Kindness can also slow aging.

Sam: Isn't it interesting, when love and kindness are received into the body, or is given, the body naturally responds by moving toward life and health!

Constance: Our bodies tell the story of what we came from, and what we are. I love the name of your show. We literally *are* love! It's an undeniable fact, backed by simple science.

Sam: Spiritual teachers have taught that we live from two energy spaces. One is love. The other is fear. What is the effect on us, from a physical standpoint, of fear?

Constance: There are the good, necessary things that happen when we sense we're in genuine danger. We get what we need in that moment: Heart rate and blood pressure increase, pupils dilate so you can see the threat more clearly. Fight-or-flight type stuff. It's been essential for our survival as a species. Especially early on. We may know it now as more of an uneasy intuitive sense of something not feeling right or safe.

Sam: Still necessary when we're sensing danger.

Constance: Yes, but fear is also a source of what takes life away.

Sam: Let's talk more about that, but we can also think of anger as only "bad." Can there be two sides to anger as well?

Constance: Absolutely. As an African American woman, I'm intrigued by history being full of people who accomplished great things in and through their anger. Social justice being one important area. People standing up for themselves, as a group, or for another group of people. People refusing to be abused.

Love can and does use any and everything. Any and everything inevitably *serves* love, I believe.

Sam: Doesn't it remind us that we're complex creatures as humans, and life is complex? It also brings me to the fact that fear or anger aren't our life's source, or our truest energy space, where life evolves to its greatest potential.

Constance: Agreed. Only love gives us the life, the oxygen we desire and need. Martin Luther King Jr. had it right when he said, "Hate begets hate, violence begets violence. Toughness begets a greater toughness. We must meet the forces of hate with the power of love." But it's very hard to sustain any effort if anger is our only fuel. We wear out over time, and people naturally resist and become defensive when we're angry. Love has an infinite supply of energy.

Sam: When I've spent time observing myself when I judge someone, I've found fear in my judgment. There is fear that the person isn't what I want them to be, and I can't change them. Fear that what I judge someone for, I'm actually seeing in myself, and I fear that I'm unable to change myself.

Constance: That's good insight for us all, Sam. Judgment is another child of fear. When we judge someone, or judge a circumstance as only "bad," our judgment triggers the body's stress response, which I just mentioned. Judgment disrupts sleep. Judgment's stress weakens the immune system, making us more susceptible to illness. It damages relationships, which takes us away from the physical benefits of positive relationships.

Sam: Again, we're back to those two energy spaces we live from: fear and love. I've felt how love *gives* life, and fear takes it away.

Constance: Yes! You could say that love is literally a homecoming. A returning to the life Source.

Again, our bodies are literally reminding us all the time of our greatest truth. Our bodies serve us as reminders of what your guest's tattoo said last week, *"you are love."*

You know, Sam, I'd like to add one more thing going back to the conversation about judging. There is something I absolutely love telling people.

People ask me the same question we're all asked. "What do you think of Jennifer," for example. I've grown into saying, "I think Jennifer does a better job of being Jennifer than anyone I know!" And I try and leave it there.

I love how my body's response lets me know that I'm in tune with life. It feels so relaxed. It seems to smile, in a way that I don't feel when I offer my precious opinions, my judgments, that are often grounded in an amazing lack of information.

Our bodies clearly tell us that we are here to be ourselves, and to accept others as they are.

Sam: We usually first think of love as something we give to someone else. But loving ourselves is vital to our being whole. What and where's the balance there?

Constance: Great question. I think it's really the *first* question to ask when we look at having love in our lives at all. The balance of self-care is absolutely crucial. It's often said, "You can't give away what you don't have."

There's a reason they tell you on airplanes to put your own oxygen mask on first, before you assist others.

Most of us grew up being taught that thinking of yourself first is selfish. Actually, "self-care first" creates the possibility of being selfless. And we do experience a richness of life when we're selfless that is absolutely delicious. But first comes the loving of yourself.

Sam: The word "love" reminds me of a dear, elderly friend, whose love for his wife of many years is such a beautiful story. He wrote an entire book of poems about the love of his life.

Constance: Oh, that's so sweet! Oh, that we'd all be so lucky!

Sam: Exactly! I once asked him how his grief at her passing changed him. He said his pain drove him back into community. He became more outgoing. He found a new love for meeting people. Finding out about them. Talking with them, but mostly listening to their stories. Through it all he said he became alive again. Actually, in a way he hadn't known before.

Constance: Beautiful story. It just shows us all is One. Made for connection. Community. Made of the love that birthed us. Everything serves love in the end, as I said before. Even the pain. Often times, *especially* the pain. If we choose to use it that way.

Your friend could have chosen to isolate even more. And the consequences of isolation are enormous. They clearly move us away from life. Isolation brings increased risk of heart disease, stroke, obesity. Isolation weakens our immune system, can increase dementia, and increase the possibility of an earlier death.

Sam: Constance, for those not familiar with your column, why do you call it Life's Labyrinth?

Constance: Oh, it's quite simple really. In a labyrinth, we walk and walk until we reach the center. I love the simple quote of spiritual teacher Ram Dass that you mentioned last week. "We're all just walking each other home."

Love is our one and only true home. Our center. *The* center. Everything revolves around it. It often takes a lot of walking in this life. A lot of searching and going after things that don't lead us home, before we reach our true center. Love.

I'm sure you're best friend here brings you home every day.

Sam: Ha! Every day! Constance Delauria, thank you so much for being with us. It has been an honor and privilege to connect with you. You are love.

Next week my guest will be Dr. Joanne McCarthy. We'll be talking about criminology and our divine nature. Say what? See you next Sunday. Remember: "We're all just walking each other home." You are love.

Carly: *And we're off.*

In the evening, Sam lit a fire and cozied up in the den. He was expecting a call from Sol. As program manager, he had formed a focus group. Five women and five men. Various ages, races, backgrounds. Sol had begun meeting online with them after the show, getting their feedback, and sharing it with Sam.

His cell rang, and true to form, Sol got right to it. "The show's off to a good start, Sam. They've loved the content of the first two episodes. They have a favorable response to you. They like how comfortable and relaxed you make them feel. Eight of them said they appreciate that you aren't talking about any one particular religion, or religion at all for that matter. They like the inclusivity of the conversation. Two said they wished you talked more in Christian terms. Eight reiterated that they're looking for content that is different than anything they would normally find on Sunday morning, spiritual programming.

"There was a reasonable uptick on viewership from the first week. All in all, it seems we're on track. Let's talk more this week."

And with that, no nonsense, Sol hung up.

Sam was taken back by how abruptly the call ended, even if it was Sol. He started to wonder if his dad felt what he was feeling now, when he so abruptly ended their conversation.

He sat back, looked around the den, and knew what he had to do. He needed to do what his own father had done. *Start* a conversation with a son who, he was convinced, didn't want to see him.

I'm starting to see now that I've carried
around this huge empty hole in me my whole life.
A hole that needed to be filled with one
thing, and one thing only. Love

7

On the Way Back to Ben

AS CHARLIE RAV4 DUTIFULLY ROLLED DOWN the road bringing Sam to Ben's college basketball practice, there was once again a lot riding on him.

There was a replaying of that precious moment he first held Ben. He saw himself looking through tears into Ben's curious, little eyes. "Hey, little guy. I've been waiting to meet you. I'm your father! Want to shoot some hoops?" The word "father" instantly plunging him into the deep end of joy, the depths of which he didn't know was possible. And giving him the dread of giving any of Frank Crawford to *his* son.

He had often wondered why some children are blessed with a good father and others are not. Was it just luck? One big crapshoot? Preordained?

He thought of how he and Ben were inseparable "best buds" when Ben was growing up. He felt again how he just couldn't get enough of Ben's . . . everything. The touch of his soft cheek. The story of life's greatest truths being told in his eyes and in his giggles. "My God, there's no better sound in the world!" he'd often say to Jadyn.

When his "dada" came home, Ben would run to the door, giggling with outstretched arms, yelling, "Surprise!" Which always prompted the thought, *Not really a surprise, buddy. We meet like this every day, but I love it!*

Sam's favorite place in the world was on Ben's bed reading stories at night, giving his son what he never had. The deep joy he felt always invited another little boy. One who was 6'8", and still needed a story he could fall asleep to.

As he grew older, Ben loved shooting into his Fisher Price basketball hoop with his dada. An orange hoop that got higher and higher, until one day reaching the normal height of ten feet on their garage. Which coincidentally was how tall his dada had seemed for as long as Ben could remember. As he drove, his heart sank. *Oh, how I miss those days. My buddy.*

He remembered how they spent hours on their driveway. A father and son finding the one thing they were *really* there for. Connection. Men are funny that way. They always have to be *doing* something together to try and find it. Maybe that's why these often-lonely beings have fewer friends. It takes too much effort. He shook his head. *All Jadyn and her friends need is a phone, or a cup of coffee!*

And there it was. BAM! He was suddenly watching the horror show of the day Sam had to tell his sixteen-year-old son the reason he had to leave.

"Ben, I've made a horrible mistake. I did something I never thought I'd do. Something I *vowed* never to do. I've . . . I've . . . there's no way to say this, other than to just say it. During the Covid lockdown, I started FaceTiming with a teacher friend of mine. I was thinking I just needed someone to talk with who understood what it was like trying to teach online, and all that brings. Well . . . I went too far with it . . . much too far."

He felt he owed it to Ben to look him in the eye when he said, "I had an affair with her."

There are no words to describe both the look on Ben's face, and how deeply it cut into the heart they once shared. It was a look Sam knew too damn well. The same look he gave his father, over and over. The look of heart-shattering disappointment and shame. The look of something as vital as oxygen being denied to you, as you feel the breath going out of your body.

"I've hurt your mom so badly. I've hurt you and let you and Avery down in indescribable ways. Ben, I'm so, so, sorry."

Ben just shot straight up. "You're not the dad I thought you were!" he screamed before running upstairs. A trip Sam had taken so many times because of his father. From upstairs, Ben Crawford began introducing his father to his new life. A life Sam knew well. Only this time, *he* was the one standing below.

The days, weeks, and months that followed were pure hell. The only communication being the daggers shooting out from Ben's eyes, penetrating the most vulnerable places in Sam's psyche.

It had been three years since that awful day, which corresponded to the amount of time Sam had spent going over and over what he was about to say to his "buddy," Ben.

As Charlie RAV4 was doing its thing, Sam rehearsed one more time. When he was done, he got to thinking about hearing his dad's ninth step. Thoughts overwhelmed Sam of how life can be like one big loop for families. Stories lived out in one generation, come back to be lived again. With nuances known only in the next generation.

He thought about his father telling him that he wanted to be there for him, but didn't want to upset him, or be the embarrassment that he was to himself. He thought about how he felt the same going to Ben's games after the affair. *You did show up, Crawford. You're showing up again. Give yourself that.*

"Even a loop can begin to find its end," became the mantra that drove him.

The moment he opened the door to the arena, Sam could feel his anxiety rising over how Ben would react to seeing him. As he walked he remembered the first conversation he had with Tim last summer at Ole's Tavern. They were talking about how the profound and meaningful is found in the things we *can't not* do. He heard Tim asking him, "What can't you *not* do, Sam?" He saw himself looking out the window, saying, "I *can't not* love my kids."

This is what it looks like for me, Sam thought to himself. With part of him wondering if he'd done the right thing by coming, and the other part absolutely knowing that he can't *not* do this. Sometimes the Good wolf within is fed enough to sit down on an arena's seat to watch your son.

"Listen up! Let's run that again!" Ben's coach yelled after a whistle blow. *God, coaches must go to whistle-blowing school,* Sam thought. *Why does it sound so sharp when they blow it?*

"Crawford, you're too slow! I need you to come out quicker and closer to your man on the perimeter!"

Sam always admired how coachable Ben was. He seemed to never get upset with the coach. He found himself wishing he had been more like that when he played. He was often muttering something under his breath to the coach.

Sam did see a lot of himself in Ben. Along with his 6'6" frame, Ben did many things like his father. He just did them in his own way, and better. He was a better defender, and a better shooter from the outside. He played bigger, faster, and stronger.

But his deepest admiration was reserved for the *person* Ben was. He watched how his son interacted with his teammates. Giving them encouragement. A smile. He heard his father again, as if he were sitting next to him, looking at him.

> *Please know, Sam, there were so many times I looked at you, and saw the person I wanted to be.*

At a break, Ben looked up, saw his dad, and there it was. A nod. The nod. And there you have it. Maybe Crawford loops *can* find their end!

After practice, Sam waited outside the locker room. When Ben came out, Sam moved toward Ben like Shadow moved toward him that first day. One cautious step, and then another. When Sam felt it was okay, he gave Ben a hug and felt what she must have felt in their embrace. Hope. What does hope feel like? Home. A home you've dearly missed for far too long.

"So good to see you, son. Sorry for just showing up without letting you know. I'm sure you're busy, but you got time for a Coke?"

"Um. Yeah. I got a couple of hours."

The Heart of the Conversation

Sam hated the awkwardness. Mostly because it reminded him of his own father trying to make conversation with him years ago. But for Sam, it was different and worse. For years he had known closeness and connection with Ben. Something Frank Crawford had never known. Short questions were followed by even shorter answers.

Searching for something, Sam blurted out, "Grandpa Crawford visited me a couple of weeks ago. He's been going to a new AA group. He wanted to share his ninth step with me. He needed to acknowledge the harm he's caused."

"Grandpa Crawford? Really?"

The thought then hit Sam like never before. *Oh Ben, you've never known my dad, your own grandfather. I'm so sorry.*

"I know I've never told you anything about what it was like growing up around him. I'll just say it was tough reliving everything. But I respect him for doing it. He told me he wanted to see what our relationship could be moving forward. I told him that I knew how hard this was for him, but I needed some time."

Tears started to well up. Tears he no longer wanted to hide. "Ben, I'm starting to see now that I've carried around this huge hole within me. It's like I always felt this empty gap between me and what I've longed for. It started when I was a little kid, and it can only be filled with one thing, and one thing only. Love."

Ben stared down at the table, holding his head in his hands, not saying a word in response.

"Ben, I'm so sorry for the hurt you've been carrying because of me. I've caused so much pain for your mom, you, and Avery, and I take full responsibility for my enormous mistake."

He leaned across the table toward his son. "I want what my dad wants. To see what our relationship could be now. I know it can never be the same. But maybe, I don't know, maybe it could be . . . I don't know what it could be, but I'd love to find out."

Ben's eyes then gave his dad a warning of what was coming. "I don't know . . . what was . . . I just can't find it. Like you said, it's not the same. I still see the hurt in Mom whenever your name is mentioned." Ben took a second to pause. He looked away. "Can't handle that."

Ben took a long, deep breath that Coach Jenkins would have been proud of and looked out the window across campus. "I don't know. What you said to your dad about needing time. Same with me."

"I get it, Ben, and you got it. Can I still come to see you? Talk sometimes? Maybe come watch you play?"

Ben thought about it. "Yeah. I'm cool with that."

They walked together out to Sam's car. As Sam got in, he heard, "Dad?"

"Yeah, Ben?" Sam quickly said, eager to take in any scrap of hope thrown at him.

"Just want you to know . . . I'll try."

"Can't ask for anything more, Ben. I love you. Be kind to yourself."

As Sam and Charlie RAV4 drove away, Ben watched them, wondering where all this was heading. He couldn't hear what his dad was thinking:

> *He's gonna try! He's gonna try!*
>
> *Sam, there have been so many times I looked at you and saw what I wanted to be.*
>
> *Ben, there have been so many times . . .*

When Sam returned home, there was no creature on earth more suited to greet him than the one jumping on him at the door. Her tail that never lied, bouncing up and down, as she felt and licked the bitter wounds of hope still waiting.

Sam's Shadow followed him into the den, and began administering massive amounts of oxytocin by putting her head on Sam's lap and staring at him.

It was time once again for their little book club. The one that met whenever their eyes did. Sam's eyes told Shadow of everything that had just transpired. A reading of hers was telling him, *I'm here. Let it be.*

8

Charlie!!!

SOMETIMES A WALK YOU TAKE EVERY DAY can bring you to where you had no intention of going. On his way to a marketing meeting the following Tuesday, Sam left his desk and walked past the news studio, deciding to stop in to watch the noon news.

The story being told was of an eighteen-year-old young woman who was killed that morning by a suspected drunk driver, just a block from the station. It was the phrases "ran a red light" and "struck the driver's side door" that took Sam away. Away to a hot June afternoon that never seemed to end.

Three weeks after their high school graduation, Sam and Charlie had planned to work out and shoot some hoops. Sam called Charlie and told him he'd be thirty minutes late. Charlie stayed home for a while and then left for the gym. As he crossed the intersection a block from the fitness center, a driver in a white Ford 4x4 blew a red light and slammed into the driver's side door of Charlie's car. Police later estimated he was going around sixty miles per hour.

Sam took the same route and came upon the scene minutes after the crash. When he saw the car, he knew. The OSU bumper sticker and the "Proud Parent of a National Honors Student" decal on the corner of the back windshield told him his best friend was in serious trouble.

He pulled over and ran as fast as he could to Charlie. A policeman grabbed him. "Stay back, son. Get back in your car. Now!"

"But that's my best friend!" Sam yelled while pulling his arm away from the officer. "I have to get to him!"

"I'm sorry, son. You have to get back to your car!"

"No! No! No!" Sam kept screaming as he headed back. From his car, with his fist pounding the steering wheel, Sam saw the first responders beginning to get out the Jaws of Life, to try and get Charlie out of the mangled mess that was his mother's car.

Sam watched in horror as they gently pulled Charlie from the vehicle and quickly brought him into a waiting ambulance. With the siren blaring, all Sam could think about was following it to the hospital. *Oh my God! Oh my God! This can't be happening! I'm right behind you bro! Right behind you!*

As he tried to follow, flashes of his life with Charlie appeared. He saw the time they first met on the playground in second grade playing four square. He saw them hanging out in Charlie's bedroom and family room, playing games or watching sports in the den. Charlie was rarely over at Sam's, for fear of how his father would show up that day.

He saw the time in third grade when they wanted to pretend they were smoking, so they rolled up pieces of construction paper and lit them, wishing they hadn't.

There were scenes of them as teenagers sneaking down to the park, or the river, to drink liquor they "borrowed" from their parents.

Sam saw the ambulance speed through a red light with its lights flashing and siren blaring. Forced to stop, he pounded his fist on the steering wheel at the light. *Goddamn fuckin' light! C'mon!* He got to the hospital a few minutes after the ambulance. He ran through the emergency door and up to the desk. "I've got to see my friend! He was just driven here by ambulance. There was an accident!"

"They're tending to him now. Please take a seat. Do you know how we can reach his parents?" A number he had called a thousand times just wasn't there. "Ah . . . seven . . . six . . . Shit! Seven . . . six . . ." Finally the numbers came.

Sam couldn't sit down. All he could do was pace around and around in the waiting room.

Carol and Walt, Charlie's mom and dad, came rushing in. Carol saw Sam and screamed, running over and hugging him. Sam held on to them both, as if doing so would make this all go away. Carol clung to Sam as if he were the only thing that was real in a very foggy nightmare. Walt was having what felt like an out-of-body experience. An attending nurse came out and told them what they were doing with Charlie.

Twenty-five years later, actually minutes, the attending emergency physician came out. She sat down, put her hand on Carol's knee, looked her in the eye, and told her everything she didn't want to hear without saying a word.

"No! No!" yelled Walt.

"I'm so sorry, Mr. and Mrs. Finnegan. Your son suffered a massive blow to his head. His heart stopped in the ambulance. It stopped again as we were getting him into the trauma room. We did everything we could." She leaned slowly toward them. "He's gone."

It was then that something like lightning cut through to Sam's core. He saw a mother's heart, so filled with love for her child, that it could not take in the doctor's words. Strange words telling her that the life she carried within her, a bond that was only hers to know, was gone.

He saw the look in her eyes telling the physician, "No. That's not possible. It cannot be true. Stop speaking to me!"

Then Sam witnessed Walt turning his wife's head toward him, as if something else were doing the turning. He saw Walt put both his hands on his wife's cheeks, put his head on her forehead, and whisper, "Oh, sweetheart."

Then Sam saw, for the first time, the raw core of a father's heart breaking. Through tears he held his wife's face again. "Sweetheart, did you hear? Charlie didn't make it. He's gone!"

After a few questions that no one remembered, the physician said, "The chaplain is on his way." Carol then muttered something about wanting to talk to her son.

After the doctor left, Sam sat in the fog with his second mom and the man he considered his father. In the silence. In the disbelief. Sam kept thinking, *He just left the house ninety minutes ago!*

Sam looked over at Carol again, and saw it all unfold in slow motion. He witnessed the horror of the truth beginning to enter her consciousness. Her face that had been like a concrete dam began showing its cracks. First the tears began welling up, and then the dam broke open, releasing the immeasurable force of a mother's fury it could no longer hold back.

"NO! NO! NO! MY CHARLIE! OH MY GOD!!!"

Walt immediately held her. Sam rushed over and put his big hands on both of them. There they were, alone in the river's torrent.

Walt got up knowing what he had to do, and made a call to his sister, Emily. He hadn't been close to her for several years. But Emily was a kind soul, and that he needed. Now.

Sam also did something that surprised him. After sitting in his car for an hour in the hospital parking lot, staring blankly ahead, he knew he couldn't go home. Instead he drove straight to the gym, driving through that horrible intersection, now cleared out as if nothing had happened.

He screamed from inside the car, "GODDAMMIT! Don't you people know what just happened here? My best friend was just fucking killed! Right here! Don't you care?"

No one heard him as they kept driving through, thinking about the phone call they needed to make. The grocery stop that needed to happen. Looking forward to dinner with a friend.

At the fitness center, in his own kind of "out of body" disbelief, it felt like he was watching himself walk into the gym. He sat down on a chair by the side of the court, staring. Occasionally looking up and seeing him and Charlie out there. Doing their thing. One-on-one. Just another day.

One-on-one was always tough for both of them because they both knew what the other was going to do. But on this horrible day, his lifelong friend made a surprise move, and Sam Crawford wasn't there in time to defend his best friend.

That night it was like Sam had never fallen asleep before. Not like this. Charlie came to him in a dream. A dream unlike any other in how *real* it felt. Sam was shooting hoops, and Charlie came up behind him. Sam turned and Charlie said, "I'm okay." He kept saying, "I'm okay. Tell my mom and dad. Tell my mom and dad."

When Sam awoke, it was all there within him, replaying itself in an odd space of peace. Remembering what Charlie had told him, he got dressed and went over to what he had often thought of as home.

"I don't know what to make of it, but it was so real," he told Charlie's mom. "And Charlie looked just fine. He was smiling and calm. He really wanted you to know he was okay. He kept saying, 'Tell my mom and dad I'm okay!' "

Carol and Walt sat on the sofa, listening. After her sleepless night in hell, an exhausted mother took great comfort in the telling. It felt to her as if it was the first thing that had really gotten through to her. "I believe that's real, Sam. Thank you." She looked over at Charlie's picture on the fireplace mantel and yelled, "But I just want him *here!*"

In the look Walt Finnegan gave him, Sam could tell he was thinking about the dream. Walt raised his shoulders toward his shaking head, as if to say, "Maybe!?"

"Coulda, woulda, shoulda." These are three brutal companions replacing your best friend after his death.

I could've stopped watching that stupid show! I would've never watched it if my dad hadn't been late coming home with his car. I should've just asked Charlie to pick me up. That's all it would have taken. Just a few seconds' difference and none of this . . .

Horrendous, relentless thoughts that can haunt you for a lifetime. Appearing out of nowhere. Driving, shopping, taking a shower, trying to fall asleep. In a TV station's news studio.

When Sam suddenly realized where he was, he found himself hearing a story about an event that was being held by the local chapter of MADD—Mothers Against Drunk Driving. It was KLUV's vision to continue to tell the story of lives forever changed.

On the monitor he watched an interview with a mother, Jennifer McDermott, who had lost her daughter, Haley, to a drunk driver. She spoke of the horror, and how her involvement with MADD was the beginning step to her healing, if that word can ever enter the conversation. It was her first step in walking toward purpose and meaning. She said she's got more walking to do.

Sometimes a walk you take every day can bring you to where you had no intention of going.

9

You Are Love
Always a Prior Story

SAM'S PRIOR LIFE WAS NOW PAYING him some visits at KLUV. The following day he saw the envelope on his desk. A letter with the name *Kelly Gronkowski* on the return address. Sam somehow knew it was *that* Kelly. The student he so worried about. The one who often triggered in him thoughts of his high school teacher Ms. Bell, as she walked into his classroom carrying her load.

Sitting down at his desk, he opened the envelope and pulled out the letter.

Dear Mr. Crawford,

Hi! My mom was watching your show, and brought me into the room. It was great to see you! I was so surprised.

The reason I'm writing is to tell you that I screwed up with some stuff last summer, and ended up at Benson Residential Center for Teens for thirty days. It's a residential facility for teens with mental, emotional, and behavioral issues.

They do individual and group therapy, as well as family therapy. I hated it at first, but then I started to really like the staff, and some of the girls I met there. We really connected.

It was so hard, but I began allowing myself to respect and love myself.

I'm back home now, and my parents and I are working through a lot of stuff. But most of all, I know it's up to me. It's so hard every day, but I know I can do this.

I just wanted you to know that you were part of what got me to where I am today. When I was at Benson, I often thought about how you always made me feel what I felt at Benson: safe, seen, heard, and that I mattered. Just you asking me how I was doing showed me you really cared. It got me through lots of hard days.

I'm thinking now that I really want to be a counselor someday at a place like Benson.

Thank you so much, and I'm so excited for you and your new job.

Kelly Gronkowski

Sam put down the letter, and sat back in his chair. A feeling of humility, gratitude, and happiness for Kelly filled him. He replayed those brief conversations he had with Kelly before and after class. *It all mattered!*

Taking out a pen and paper, he wrote his response.

Dear Kelly,

What a wonderful surprise to find your letter on my desk this morning! Thank you so much for taking the time to write to me.

I'm so happy for you! You're just beginning to remember your truth, and she is amazing!

I always saw so much love and talent in you. I saw your tender heart. Your compassion was always there in the empathy you were feeling for other students.

If you do choose to one day be a counselor, you will be a terrific one.

I would love to continue to hear about what you're doing with your life as you discover your truth. Your true self.

You are love,
Mr. Crawford

It was Kelly's letter that carried him to the following Sunday's show.

Carly: *And five, four, three . . .*

Sam: Good morning, everyone, and welcome to KLUV's *You Are Love*. A show where we air our belief in *you*—that you are love at your core. Your essence. I'm your host, Sam Crawford. And this is Shadow. Someone who is love, every day. Thanks for being with us, Shadow.

Shadow looks up from her spot next to Sam's foot, with a look that says, "Just doing my job!"

If you're a first-time viewer of this show, or of KLUV, it is our vision to lift up the human spirit.

If you've caught one of our news broadcasts, you may have noticed that on our news at noon, six, and ten, we often tell stories of people responding to tragedy with love, healing, and purpose. But at the same time, we don't want to bury our heads in the proverbial sand and ignore the tragic realities of life.

Our show today is about putting tragedy in a broader perspective, without denying its horror. We can so easily get lost, even consumed, in the tragedy itself that we lose sight of the fact that it often has a prior story that created it. And what is within that prior story can perhaps move us to respond with some measure of compassion and love.

I welcome our guest this morning, Joanne McCarthy. Dr. McCarthy has three doctorates. One in criminal justice, a doctor of divinity degree, and a doctorate in metaphysics. She is an associate professor at Buford University, outside of Newcastle.

She is a well-known speaker and lecturer on the topic of metaphysics. Good morning, Dr. McCarthy.

Joanne: Good morning. Thank you for having me. Please call me Joanne. And Shadow, thank you for being here.

Shadow gets up as the dutiful cohost that she is, and licks Joanne's hand.

Sam: That's an interesting combination of doctorates: criminology, divinity, and metaphysical science.

Joanne: I seek to understand *why* people do what they do. From their light *and* from their darkness.

Sam: Would you explain to our viewers what metaphysical science is?

Joanne: Sure. Metaphysics means "after the physical." It examines what cannot be reached after the objective study of physical reality. What cannot be known in the five senses. It's a study of the spiritual root of physical life. Of existence itself.

Sam: We see in the news stories of violence, hate, and anger, culminating in extreme acts like mass shootings or school shootings. Bullying appears to be on the rise as a form of power. Can you help us get to the metaphysical or spiritual root of what we're experiencing in our country?

The Heart of the Conversation

Joanne: I'll begin by going back to what you talked about with your guest in your first show. I do so because I see this as fundamentally a *spiritual* issue, with spiritual roots. As all things ultimately are. Your guest talked about our souls all emerging out of the one common Source. Its essence of love flowing within all that is. This connection is innate.

It is known and remembered by the soul, and is as crucial as breath is to our bodies. This knowing is always there within the soul, whether *we* are aware of it or not, as human beings. When we are *consciously aware* of living in that truth, we, and all life thrives.

When we're not consciously aware of living in that truth, there is great pain, and we act out that pain, either toward those around us, or ourselves.

Sam: You say, *consciously* aware.

Joanne: The truth of our natural Oneness is always there. If you don't believe it, Oneness still exists. It's our awareness of it, or not, that determines how we live.

Sam: Are you saying that *feeling* lack of love and being *unaware* of connection are fundamental reasons for these acts of violence?

Joanne: Yes, I am. Every person and situation is unique and often complex. But *generally* speaking, whether we're talking about a bully, someone lost in hate, or a mass or school shooter, there is a common denominator. And that is a *conscious* lack of connection and love. It's the deepest, most visceral pain we can know as humans, because it violates our most basic, fundamental truth. And lack of love will lead to lack of self-love.

You mentioned bullying as a form of power. A bully is actually feeling power*less,* weak, afraid, and insecure. And it scares the hell out of them. All of which is fundamentally fed by lacking any sense of connection and love.

Either with someone central in their lives, like a parent, or love for themselves.

Something in them knows they have worth and value. They desperately want someone to see it, acknowledge it, but no one has. Again, the isolation of that violates the inherent, natural Oneness. This causes an overwhelming, visceral pain they want to inflict onto everyone around them.

Sam: You bring to mind a TedTalk I watched on YouTube called "I Was Almost a School Shooter" by Aaron Stark. He grew up being told he was worthless. That he would never amount to anything. He was bullied for being fat. He eventually got a gun, and was all set to shoot up either his school that day, or a food court. He said it didn't matter. "Maximum damage" was all he cared about. He wanted to do something proportional to his pain.

He said one person that day treated him "like a person," as he put it. Just asked to hang with him a little. That was all it took for him to not follow through with his plan.

Joanne: Hmmm. Can't help but look at Shadow when you say that. Yes, I saw that TedTalk too. One person showing him a bit of love. And what did it do? It brought him back into his Truth with a capital T. And the truth of all reality. The truth of a Oneness in a love he was always a part of, but had become unaware of by receiving everything *but* love.

Sam: I believe that kindness shown to Aaron came from a person whom Aaron had treated poorly. Aaron said, "Love the ones who you feel deserve it the least, because they *need* it the most. It will help you just as much as it will help them."

Joanne: They need it the most, because they've violated their own core truth. You look at Dylan Klebold, the Columbine shooter. At fifteen he began to withdraw. He wrote in his diary: *I hate my life, I want to die . . . [I have] a nice family, a good house.*

But it was his lack of peer connection that troubled him. He wrote that he had a couple of good friends. But no girl. Nobody accepting him, even though he wanted to be accepted. He made a list of all the people he loved, who would never love him back.

Something was broken in his natural chain of connection with himself and others.

And when that is broken, or *perceived* to be broken, there is great pain. We're going to act out in anger, as if we're trying desperately to breathe and get back to the oxygen of this fundamental truth our souls need to live and thrive.

Here are some wise words from an African proverb:

"A child who is not embraced by the village will burn it down to feel its warmth."

Sam: Oh my. That takes my breath away.

Joanne: If Aaron would have acted out that day, it would have ironically been an attempt to return to his fundamental truth: connection. For community. For Oneness.

Sam: A wanting for someone to see their pain.

Joanne: Precisely. Visceral pain is our deep truth teller, telling us that something profound is being violated.

Sam: What can be done to change the narrative?

Joanne: I recently heard a talk from a former police officer who now works with the University of Colorado Center for Study and Prevention of Violence. He said violence prevention is not a simple problem with a simple answer. He quoted H. L. Mencken: "For every complex problem there is an answer that is clear, simple, and wrong."

We like to think that technical solutions will solve school shootings: clear backpacks so you can see what's in them, one entrance into the school, metal detectors, more armed officers. Even arming teachers.

He said all these things can be part of a *comprehensive* strategy that we can agree or disagree with, but there is much more to it.

Sam: Whoa. As a high school teacher of twenty years, I can tell you that teachers vehemently resist the notion of being armed. No one went into teaching to carry a gun. I would have left years ago if that had ever happened. We have to be willing to get at the deeper, spiritual reasons and truths that dictate human behavior. It will call each of us to be part of the solution in ways that will often challenge us.

Joanne: Exactly. I think of the parents who are out there in schools, telling the stories of their own children's suicides from bullying. They say the number one thing kids are telling them is, they need adults in their life who will *listen* to them. Validate what they're feeling.

Again, we're back to that fundamental truth of connection and love—in this case through listening. It's hard not to, but parents tend to either tell kids to ignore the bullying, or they want to go to the school and *fix* it some way. And the kid will always say, "Don't do that! It will just make it worse." Which is why seventy-five percent of kids don't talk to an adult when they're struggling.

Sam: So what does a parent, who's just trying to love their child, do?

Joanne: All the research shows that its peers who have the power. Peer power. By the age of eighteen, the average kid spends eleven thousand hours in school. Much more than they do with their parents. When peers intervene, within ten seconds the bullying often stops. A simple "Are you okay?" from a peer is powerful. "Come hang out with me. Sit with me." It's the power of peer connection.

That's a conversation parents can have with their kids—encouraging them to look out for that kid who looks like they're struggling, looks isolated, and to reach out to them.

I don't mean to lecture parents, but a good question for all of us parents is a simple one. Am I a good listener? Am I asking questions instead of only trying to fix?

When adults don't listen, the son or daughter feels unheard. Isolation is a profound violation of the core truth of ourselves and reality: Oneness. Connection.

Sam: This brings me to a talk I heard from Christian Picciolini. He was a former member of a gang some of us may have heard of, MS-13. He said his mother came here from El Salvador to create a better, safer life for her son. So here's a loving mother willing to make great sacrifices for her son. The problem was she had to work all the time for them to survive. So Christian was spending a lot of time alone, and in a foreign culture. We can at least imagine how difficult that was for him.

He talked about how disconnection breeds fear. He himself was bullied for being of another race. Disconnection breeds ignorance, and when we don't understand something we tend to be afraid of it.

While all that was going on, he desperately wanted to belong, which he said was the number one reason young men join gangs. So here we are again, at that fundamental truth of Oneness. Belonging. Something in us, in our core, knows it belongs. Knows it's part of something bigger than itself. But that's being violated. Ignored. Unmet. And we want to go home, so to speak. Back to knowing Oneness. Connection. So we seek that out in sometimes destructive ways.

He said that the number one reason gang members get out of the gang life is they receive an act of compassion from someone they least deserved to receive it from.

That's what happened to him. Those he had criminally violated reached out to him with compassion.

Now he's part of an organization of former gang members working to help people get out. They've helped hundreds to do just that.

It took showing compassion, a welcome, giving them a healthy community experience, and an alternative. Which puts everyone involved back into that core, fundamental truth of Oneness.

His advice for everyone in the audience? Find someone you think is undeserving of your compassion and give it to them, because they need it the most.

Joanne: Just like Aaron Stark experienced.

Sam: Yeah. What we're talking about here doesn't just apply to dramatic situations like school shootings, bullying, or gangs. It applies to many other times when we're simply treated in an unloving way. Someone is rude to us, cuts us off on the road, and honks their horn. They have a story, too.

Joanne: We're so quick to judge and only see the act, while not knowing the backstory.

I was in a fast-food restaurant the other day, and a guy came in who had been waiting in the drive-through. He started yelling at the high school kid at the counter, "I've been sitting out there for fifteen minutes waiting for a f'n hamburger!"

After I let go of my usual "What a jerk!" response, I reminded myself that it's not about the hamburger. No matter what it is, it's usually not about the thing being talked about. What else is going on in that person's life? That's the question to ask.

I stood there and sent him, and that poor kid at the counter, love. Loving thoughts of compassion and empathy, as best I could. Reminding myself that I have no idea what his life or story is. Maybe his wife just told him that morning that she's leaving him. I don't know.

Sam: It's going to take enough of us willing to go there, reaching out with compassion for those who, in our judgment, don't deserve it.

Joanne McCarthy, thank you for being with us today. What a privilege to have this extremely important conversation with you. We'll be right back.

Carly: *And we're off.*

After a couple of local stories, and music from a local band, Sam ends the show.

Sam: Thank you for being part of our community this morning. On next Sunday's show, I'll be speaking with three special guests on the subject of wisdom.

Remember: "We're all just walking each other home," and you are love.

Carly: *And we're off.*

With that, Sam headed home. On his way he checked his phone, and there was a text from Jadyn.

Sam. Would you call me? We need to talk. Thanks.

10

We Need to Talk.

***WE NEED TO TALK,* SAM THOUGHT.** Like most people, Sam had always found these words to bring things as pleasant as a colonoscopy. She might as well have added, *Samuel Franklin Crawford. We need to talk.* The only time he ever heard his full name spoken to him was from his mother, and it was never good. *Why do we do that to people?* he often wondered. *So much thought goes into choosing the full name, and then we teach them to dread hearing it!*

Sam had already planned a visit back home to see Avery on Monday, his day off. The trip began with Sam seeing one shoe lying by the side of the road, turned over on its side. He smiled as he remembered the time he and Charlie saw George Carlin perform at the local civic center. Carlin began by talking about seeing one shoe by the side of the freeway on the way to the show.

"Why is there always *one* shoe?" Carlin asked. "What? Is some schmuck driving along, looking down at his shoe, and saying, 'Well, guess I don't need *this one!*' "

They both thought it was hilarious. "It's true!" Charlie told Sam. "I've seen it!"

Sam knew that shoe well. Once part of a pair that someone had thrown away.

On the rest of the trip back home, Sam spun his stories of why Jadyn wanted to talk.

She wants to talk about Ben or Avery. But why can't we do that over the phone like we always do?

She wouldn't be moving. Not with Avery doing so well at her group home. Unless they're both moving!

Maybe she's met someone. She hasn't said anything about that. Even if she was with someone, why wouldn't she just tell me over the phone?

By the time Sam walked into the coffee shop where he and Jadyn had agreed to meet, Sam had increased the story's drama and importance, as all good storytellers do. When he saw Jadyn sitting at her little table by the window, staring out into the traffic going by, he quickly knew his stories hadn't been too far off.

He stopped for a moment, feeling again what it was like for them to be together now, or to even talk on the phone. Even though it was always about the kids, *their* story was always there, being retold in the background. The volume turned down, but still audible.

Stories of their coming together. Their plunging into each other's hearts. Their learning things about each other that no one else knew. The home they once shared in their "us." The joys and struggles that they only knew in Ben and Avery. His betrayal. And a thousand others which only they can read in each other's eyes. One glance, a novel. Pain that was only theirs to feel, live with, and begin to resolve. If only they could get to the end. Novels can be so bloody long.

"You look lost in thought," Sam said, walking toward her.

"Oh, hi, Sam. Thanks for coming."

"How are you?" It was a question whose answer he felt responsible for, knowing what he had put her through. A question asked in hopes that he could turn the page and read the chapter in her eyes about how she's really doing well, and that he hadn't totally f'd up her life.

"I'm good. Really! And you?" she said with a smile that seemed to know something.

It was then Sam felt what he had always felt with her now. That feeling of two people walking into a home they had once shared, but clearly didn't live in anymore. He paused and shrugged. "To be honest, I don't really know. Haven't really asked myself much lately.

I *think* I'm good. I'm really enjoying doing the show. It's given me a new purpose."

"I haven't watched it."

The empty feeling surprised him. He was surprised at how the instinct was still there to want what was important to him to be important to her.

"But I have a couple of friends who have, and they said it was good. That it was calming. We all need that these days. Congratulations. That's a bold leap you took there."

"Thanks. What've you been up to?" he asked. He noted again how peculiar it felt looking into the eyes of someone whose life he once felt he knew every detail of, but who was now fast becoming a stranger with a life all her own.

"I've been busy. Working. Being with Avery. Taking a lot of time to reassess everything. I haven't mentioned it when we've talked, but I've been seeing a therapist, and I really like her. She's compassionate, but no nonsense. Not afraid to challenge me. Asks the hard questions."

She leaned toward Sam. "The reason I wanted to see you was … I'm getting married. I know that's really out of nowhere for you. I guess I just needed to be with this relationship for a while, and let it be what it wants to be."

Sam didn't hear anything after "I'm getting married." He was playing the words in his head, and was taken aback by what first came to mind. His asking Jay to marry him, and his realizing he hadn't really let go of her as much as he'd thought.

The next thing he heard was "I've thought about telling you earlier, but then I realized, 'Why? It's *my* life!' " She stared at Sam for a moment. "I guess we've both had our secrets."

Now he was totally tracking. *I got it, Jay. That one was for me.*

"Anyway, I thought it best to tell you in person."

"I'm … Wow! Okay. Ah, who is he?"

Jay leaned in toward Sam again. "Sam, it's who is she? Her name is Laura."

He couldn't speak. All he could do was stare into Jay's eyes, as if he was trying to make sure he was reading the book he thought he had pulled off the shelf.

Maybe I'm not hearing this right. So he went back and read her eyes again, while rewinding and playing the tape again in his head. *No. There it is. Her name is Laura.*

"I know this has to come as a shock to you. It's why I wanted to tell you in person. I know you need some time with this. Or *is* it the shock I'm imagining it is for you?"

"Oh, you're right about the shock." Sam nodded, trying to come up with something to say. "Ah ... when did you know? I mean, about you?"

"I've known for most of my life. Growing up, I knew I could easily be in a relationship with a woman. It wasn't until college that I started to come to terms with my being bisexual."

"Okay. Context, please?"

"The nights before your games, I'd sometimes go to parties, and I experimented a little. There was a woman on our volleyball team I noticed I had real feelings for. Feelings I couldn't deny. I privately was sorting it out, and I chose to stay with you. Anyway, I can't tell you how good it feels to finally embrace my truth."

"Oh. All of that was going on with you all along? And I had no idea?" He then almost shouted something more directed at himself, than her. "I had no idea!"

"As I said, we both have had our secrets. Interesting, isn't it?"

"Yeah," Sam said, seeing he had no credibility in the "Why didn't you tell me?" department. He kept shaking his head. "All this time."

He looked out the window, as if looking into his heart, and was grateful for the compassion he saw there. Turning to Jadyn, he said to the woman he'd thought he had fully known for twenty-two years, "What was that like to live with? For so long?"

"Thanks for asking. Lonely. Confusing at times. Before Laura, I've really only ever talked about it with two girlfriends. One in high school, and one in college."

Jadyn put her hand on Sam's arm. "Sam, what we had was real. I wasn't faking anything. There's just this whole other side to me that I'm finally allowing myself to accept and welcome." She sat back and shook her head. "It's been a long road, to say the least."

She let her ex-husband have his time. His space. After about ten minutes of a one-minute silence, Sam said, "Tell me about her."

Just like that, a light came on in Jadyn that Sam couldn't miss. "I met Laura at a party of a mutual friend of ours about two years ago," she said, smiling. "We were just two people who needed someone to talk to. She was coming off a divorce too. We both quickly knew that we had found in each other what we had been looking for, for a very long time."

That one hurt, Sam thought, feeling like he had never been enough.

"The friendship grew, and well, here we are. Getting married in three months! She's amazing, Sam. Laura is insightful, funny, loves life, and is so compassionate. She listens, and when she does, I feel a connection with her that's on a level I've never known. We understand each other as women. Anyway, like I said, it feels so good to love myself so authentically."

"Does Ben know?"

"He's known for about a year now. He's met Laura. Ben's been amazing. He's actually happy for me."

"Not surprised."

"Me either."

"Avery?"

"Laura's come with me when I go see Avery. So far I've told her that Laura is my good friend. Avery has been Avery about it all. She likes Laura. They've really hit it off."

"Again, not surprised. Well, looks like I've ah . . . got some catching up to do here."

"I understand. I just hope, for the sake of Ben and Avery, that you will try. Knowing you, I believe you will. But then again . . . uncharted territory, and all that."

"Thank you for saying that, Jadyn Cecilia Calloway." Sam had often said her full name whenever she had said or done something remarkable.

Jadyn had taken back her last name, Calloway, about five years into their marriage. She was starting to feel out of touch with her story. With herself. When she first talked with Sam about her wanting to take her name back, Sam understood and supported her in every way he could in the process. He stood behind her when people judged her for it.

It was from Jadyn that Sam learned the importance and power of names. It was from her that he learned that when you honor the name, you honor the person. He saw how careful Jadyn was to make sure a woman's name was spelled and pronounced correctly. He saw how empowering it was for her to again think of herself as she had always been, and always will be. A Calloway.

"I'm not a Crawford, Sam," she told him at the time. "Crawfords aren't who made me what I am. The people in the Calloway story, *they've* made me who I am. The stories I've lived being a Calloway. That's who I am."

Jadyn Calloway "came from good people," as they say. People whose stories and lives enabled her to always turn the page to the next chapters of her life with strength and confidence. A story filled with women who stood proud with a fierce belief and love for themselves, providing her the strength and inspiration to deal with her pain after Sam's betrayal.

Her grandmother Cecilia was a wonderful woman. Sometimes people's names get lost in the generations that follow them, but not Cecilia's. It simply couldn't be. From everything Jadyn shared with him of her "grammy," Sam had always seen a lot of her in Jadyn. Cecilia was the first woman in her family to graduate from college. The first to go to graduate school and become a school principal. The first woman to run for public office. The first woman to be elected to town counsel, and eventually the first woman mayor that anyone had ever known for miles around.

Jadyn spoke often of her grammy with Sam. She told him about witnessing her swearing-in ceremony as mayor, and how badass she looked that day. How she seemed to be telling everyone that no one, especially any man, is ever going to tell her what she can and cannot be.

"Jay, for so long now, I've feared I've destroyed your happiness. But now, I don't feel like I even have to ask if you are. I can see it."

Jadyn shook her head and smiled. "You don't have that kind of power, Sam. *I'm* in charge of my well-being. I'm so proud of myself for embracing that."

And there it was. The truth she had worked so damn hard to know. The truth that could actually begin to set Sam free as well. If only he would accept it for the gift it was.

Jadyn looked out the window for a moment and smiled. "It's a different kind of happy though, one that I'm just in the process of getting to know."

"So beautiful to hear that, Jay!" He was surprised by how much he meant it. "Grammy Cecilia would be proud of you. I know I am."

The words tasted delicious as they came out of his mouth. Their authenticity like a meal he had been longing for, for a very long time. Thinking about how far he had just traveled in the last few minutes, Sam allowed himself to do something he hadn't for a very long time. He let himself be proud of Sam Crawford.

"Thanks, Sam. I thought you'd react this way. But you never know. Uncharted . . ."

"Territory," Sam said, finishing her sentence. "That's all we've been in lately, Jay."

He paused. "I know this may still be hard to believe, but I meant it before when I told you that I never stopped loving you."

"You know, Sam . . . after you left, I can't tell you how many times I asked myself if I still loved you. I hated what you did, and I knew I couldn't be with you anymore. But as hard as I tried, for some reason, I never could get myself to say, 'I don't love Sam.' I stopped loving you in the way I always had, but still, a certain kind of love remained. I felt kind of a strange, almost . . . comfort. Can't explain it."

"Thank you, Jay. That means so much to me." He reached for her hand. "I appreciate you making the effort to meet in person."

He checked the time. "Well, better get over to see our girl."

As he got up to leave, he stopped, paused, and turned around. "Could you answer me this? Looking back on everything," he said, taking a couple of steps toward Jadyn, "are you grateful for what we had?"

Jadyn stood and smiled. "I am, Sam. I truly am. The joys. The pain. Ben and Avery. All of it. Of course I am. I'm Jadyn Cecilia Calloway!"

Sam did the only thing he needed to do. He hugged her and took a half step back. "Thank you, Jay. Me too. More than you'll ever know."

When Sam got back in his car, all he could do was stare ahead. What just happened? Whatever that was, it felt strangely . . . peaceful. Yeah. That's the word.

If you asked, he couldn't have told you anything about driving over to the group home. But he must have done so, because the next thing he remembered was greeting Cheryl, the supervisor on duty.

"Hey, Sam! How are you?"

There are so many times we ask that question of someone, and we have no clue what just transpired for them. Sam had a quick recall of the guy his guest spoke of in the last show. The one at the fast-food place yelling about a hamburger. The one with a prior story.

He thought, *We really have no idea.*

In a flash he imagined himself telling Cheryl how he *really* was. Telling her everything that he and Jadyn had just talked about. Wrapping it up an hour later with, *So, that's the story of me and my ex-wife, Jadyn, whose bisexuality I learned of an hour ago. But hey, enough about me. How are you?*

He did what we all do. "I'm good, Cheryl. And you?"

"Been a good day today! Avery's been looking forward to seeing you. Right now she's downstairs working on a puzzle with Chloe. You can go down if you'd like."

"How's she been lately with her outbursts here, and at her job?"

"Yeah, that seems to have settled down. She just goes to her room. Or Jadyn comes over and settles her down. She's been bringing a friend with her who Avery just loves."

"Laura! Yes, I hear good things. I'm glad." *I hear good things. Welcome to your new life, Crawford!*

When Avery saw her dad, she shot up to give him one of her patented long hugs that have no need to stop. "Hi, Dad!"

"Oh, Avery, I'm so happy to see you! How are you?"

"Good. This is Chloe. She's my friend."

"Hi, Chloe!"

Avery's introduced Sam to Chloe before. An introduction that always feels like meeting an old friend for the first time.

"What are you two working on?"

"Puzzle."

Avery has *loved* puzzles for years. It was one of the few things she could stay with for some reason.

"Can I watch?"

"Yeah."

Whenever Sam was around Avery, he always found conversation, and life for that matter, to be refreshing. Short and to the point. Life seemed simpler. Less cluttered by all the drama her dad, and most of the population, added to everything.

"Avery. How's your job going?" Sam asked as they looked for one of the last missing pieces. She worked stuffing envelopes for mass mailings at a company about a mile from the home.

"Good. Got into trouble though."

"Yeah, I heard. What happens when you get into trouble?"

"They tell me to go to a room and breathe. Maybe watch TV or something for a while."

"Does that help?"

"Yeah. Then I work again."

Avery and Chloe put in the last missing piece and high-fived each other.

"Avery, there's a basketball game on now. You want to watch with me?"

"Sure."

Sam and Avery loved watching sports together. It didn't matter much what the sport was. She didn't care about the rules, or which team scored. She just cheered for both. She couldn't lose. She reminded him of his college teammate Booker in that way. Always looking like he was winning.

Sam admired that about her. She knew happy when she saw it. That's all that mattered to her. He also envied Avery in one special way. He watched how accepting she usually was of people. Didn't get caught up in endless commentary and judgment like he did. Which often caused him to wonder, *Who's the "challenged" one here?* He always knew the answer.

After they watched for a while, the ritual of visiting Frazier's Ice Cream Shop was in order. Sam and Avery had been going there for years. "Hey, Avery!" was always heard as they walked in. Followed by another constant. A shared banana split.

"I hear Mom has been coming to visit you with her new friend, Laura!"

"Yeah, Laura. I like Laura. She's funny. Her and I play games."

Sam smiled. "That's great." He noticed again how he really meant it. For the first time he was realizing a strange, new kind of good was beginning to appear out of everything that was so bad.

The words just came out. "Thank you, Avery."

"What?"

"Oh, nothing." *Avery,* he thought, *you have no idea just how something that "nothing" is. No. You do! You always have. I'm always the one catching up.*

As Sam was leaving her room, they hugged. Sam and the gold-medal hugger. Long ago, Avery had taught Sam that there are some things in life you just hang on to. Hugs being one of them.

When Sam got to her door, he turned around. "I love you, Avery."

"Love you too, Dad!"

When Sam got home around 9 PM, Shadow joined him in the den. Sam got a fire going, and she snuggled up to his left foot, as Sam fell exhausted into his chair. The fire's random flames dancing about, like the day's thoughts.

So much had happened in a matter of days. As the rocks from the Willoughby River began to warm the room, he felt a soothing warmth welling up within him as he relived his genuine happiness for Jadyn. He felt again her appreciation for how he responded to her. He felt again the first embrace they had shared in three years. Anything can find its warmth again. Even someone who has felt like a rock that has known the brutal cold of winter.

He saw Avery and Chloe finding that piece of the puzzle they were looking for. The one that helped complete the picture. Feeling now like he had taken another step toward finding his own. He felt the warmth of Avery's hug, and the companionship he was now sharing with Shadow.

He thought about that lone shoe, once part of a pair, lying by the side of the road. Remembering again that the "someone" who had thrown it away was him.

Staring into the fire, the flames shot upward, as if they knew of somewhere they needed to go. Each flicker, another attempt to get there. In their light, Sam saw the text he needed to send.

Dad, Sam here. We need to talk. Next Saturday?

4

11

We Need to Talk. Part Two

WHEN SAM WATCHED FRANK CRAWFORD drive away that day from Finnegan's, he didn't know where his father was headed. He wasn't sure where Sam Crawford was headed either. But on this day, he was feeling like he knew a whole lot more.

The little town, Fillmore, that was now hosting his dad, was a two-hour drive to the north of Newcastle.

The two-lane highway eventually led Sam and Shadow through wooded and hilly terrain. The fall leaves were a little past their peak. The deeper golds, reds, and shades of crimson offering a diminished look at the beauty they once proudly displayed. *If only you were here a couple of weeks ago*, they seemed to say.

Sam thought of his dad. *If only this had happened years ago.* But people are like trees, holding colors within themselves. Beautiful colors that only appear in their time.

And what was really driving Sam that Saturday was his father. This stranger who had just started to show colors he had always hoped were in there. Somewhere. True colors of honesty, humility, courage, and vulnerability. Colors just now visible, for the both of them to see. He thought of the one question before him now. *Will I show my father the same? Are they really there?*

He found himself still uncertain about what he would say to his father. His inner knowing telling him to wait and let the moment guide him. Shadow? Well, she was . . . keeping it simple. She was there.

As the trio of Sam, Shadow, and Charlie RAV4 rolled into Fillmore, the town looked like it lived up to its namesake. It had been settled by family of the former thirteenth president of the United States, Millard Fillmore. Presidential historians rank him as one of the worst presidents, describing him as weak and inept. A member of the Whig Party, Fillmore was the last president to be neither Republican nor Democrat.

Fillmore. Appropriate name for a town seemingly looking for what it was, and not thinking much of its options: a hardware store, two liquor stores, two bars, a gas station, and a laundromat that made you wonder if you'd be better off going down to the creek and beating your clothes against a rock. Three churches, a John Deere dealership, and a restaurant that looked like it made anyone think they could wait until they got home.

For Lease signs posted in the windows of empty storefronts were the only invitation to come and invest in Fillmore that Sam could see. These seemed to be the highlights the local chamber of commerce had to work with in a marketing campaign Sam began to imagine:

Fillmore. This Is It!

But then Sam saw it. At the end of a block that had been cleared out, stood a beautiful new grocery store. Looking very much like someone had believed in a future no one around it could see. Even the name spoke of it:

Hopeman's Grocery

The three drove by older homes crying for attention, and a ballpark that had a faded Home of the Wildcats sign hanging on a grandstand that looked like it would rather not have anyone come and sit on it.

Just beyond the ballpark, Sam could see the brick apartment building his father spoke of.

After pulling up, Sam and Shadow emerged, while Charlie RAV4 seemed to be thinking, *You gonna leave me here?*

Shadow was probably the first to be impressed with Fillmore for quite some time. She sniffed around, finding lots of new delights.

Sam opened a front door starved for some WD-40, and he and Shadow walked up a stairway whose steps greeted them each in their own way. Walking down the hallway, they came to apartment 4. Frank's home.

After everything Frank Crawford had gone through in his life. After all those years he shared with Betsy, Karen, and Sam in a nice two-story home, with a backyard and a basketball court. After all the hard work to provide, and that awful day he pushed his son into the wall. It had all come down to a number.

4

Sam stood at the door for a full minute, asking himself one more time, *You really want to do this?* After the knock that announced it was time, his dad opened the door.

Game On!

"Sam. Thank you so much for coming. Come in."

Shadow walked in with Sam, as if to say, *Well, if you're doing this, I am too!*

"Hi. This is Shadow."

"Hey, Shadow," Frank said, leaning over to pet her. "Ah, you're a good girl, aren't ya?"

After sniffing Frank, she looked at Sam. *Yeah, he checks out.*

"Have a seat on the couch."

Sam sat on an old couch that let him sink lower than planned. Shadow went right into her default position, nestling up against Sam's foot, and never taking her eyes off of Frank.

"I made some coffee. You want some?"

"Yeah, sure. That would be great."

"Well, not sure how great it is. Want some cream or anything?"

"No. Black is fine."

Sam looked around after Frank went into the tiny kitchen. The dreaded feeling of being back in his own awful apartment, the day he left his family, came over him. The word "sparse" would fit. Filled with nothing that would make an old, dirty, empty space a home. He did spot a picture on a small bookshelf. *Is that what I think it is?*

Shadow followed Sam. *It is!* An old photo of the only trip they had taken as a family, to Yellowstone. There they were, looking like your typical happy family, standing in front of Old Faithful. *Oh my God! It mattered to him!*

He didn't remember much about that trip, only that at night his dad would leave, saying he wanted to check out the scenery. They all knew what he was doing. Faithfully.

Sam truly had no idea. No idea of the countless times Frank sat staring at the four of them at Yellowstone. Thinking of how good it felt to be with them, but not able to say it. Beating himself up over leaving at night. Time he could have been a real father. Time he will never have back.

"Alright. Here it is, Sam. Want to sit at the table?"

"Sure."

When Shadow resumed her spot at Sam's foot, Sam asked, "So how long have you lived here?"

"Two years. It ain't much, I know. But it's what I can afford these days."

Awkward pause . . .

"Thanks for getting back to me, son. It means the world to me."

When Sam spotted the tears welling up in his dad's eyes, he felt the moment take charge, just like his inner knowing told him it would.

"I've been doing a lot of thinking since we met," Sam said. At first he was talking to the stained carpet and then looked his father in the eye. "I went through it all. The hurt. The pain. What you shared with me. Then I thought about a time last summer with my friend Tim.

The guest you saw on the first show. I needed to tell him something that was very hard for me to talk about. Probably what it was like for you sharing your ninth step.

"I told him something terrible that I had done. Something that hurt my own family, deeply. Then I remembered what my friend did." Tears started welling up in Sam's eyes. Shadow stood up and put her head on Sam's lap, and did what wise creatures do. Saying without words, *Right behind you.*

He cleared his throat. "My friend put his hand on my arm. He told me, I don't judge you." Looking into his father's eyes, he knew the time had arrived to finally set himself free from the prison he had known for far too long. "I'm done with it. I don't judge you either . . . Dad."

Forty years of tears fell. Like leaves falling in a gentle rain. Leaves that had waited their entire season to show their brilliant colors.

Without thinking about it, the two big guys in apartment 4 shot up and hugged each other for the first time since . . . well, neither of them knew. Shadow jumped up and put her paws on Sam. Then on Frank. Her bark shouting, *You did it!*

"I don't want to live like this anymore," Sam cried. "It's killing me!"

"I don't either, son."

When the two big guys were able, they sat back down, and there they were again. Sitting across a table from each other. But this time was so beautifully different. No awkward silence.

"You were right. I was embarrassed by you," Sam said, wiping his tears. "I so wanted you to be the kind of dad my friends had."

Frank took Sam's arm. "Me too, son. But I had so much anger in me."

"Anger about what?"

"Sam," Frank said. He walked over and pulled a picture out of an old photo album. "This is your grandfather."

It was then that Sam saw his grandfather for the very first time, and learned his name. Lyle.

His dad never talked about his father. When he and Karen would ask about his parents, Frank would only say, "Your grandmother. She did right by us in taking care of us. But she could be a mean woman too. She did the best she could, I guess. But my old man. That son of a bitch. I don't want to talk about him. It's good you never met him." That was all he would ever say.

Sam stared at the picture of this man who he had always wondered about. His face showed no smile. His eyes looking as if their light had gone out long ago. Frank continued, "He used to beat the shit out of me. I was so afraid of him. Kept away from him as much as possible. Now, with the work I'm finally doing, I at least understand some of his 'why,' that we talk about at meetings. He had so much pain in him. I see it now. I don't really know much of his story growing up. Just enough to know it was bad."

Frank took the picture from Sam. "And I gave you the same pain. Dammit! Sam, I'm so sorry!"

"I never knew! I never knew, Dad! I always wondered where it was coming from. I kept thinking there had to be a reason. Something!"

The moments guided them both to say a lot of things that day. Beautiful colors that were always there, like those leaves waiting to reveal themselves in their time.

"Dad, I'm so sorry for what you went through."

"Thank you, son. I don't mean to tell you about it like it's some kind of free pass. I'm learning that I still chose to be the father I was. I gotta own that. I see that now. But . . . damn. The pain. The anger was too much sometimes!"

"I know. I know, Dad."

Frank pushed through his tears. "I'm sorry you know."

A look of deep regret came over Sam's face. "And *I've* hurt my own son. He has to live with that now. I do, too. But he didn't *choose* any of it. I did."

Frank looked up from his coffee cup. "You said you did something that was tough for you to admit. Mind if I ask you what it was? I know that's your own business. But, you know."

Sam took a deep breath. "This is embarrassing. But . . . I had an affair. An affair with a teacher I worked with."

A slight smile that knew things it wish it didn't came over Frank. "I understand, Sam. I don't judge you, son," Frank said. He put his hand on Sam's arm. Sam shook his head, amazed at this second visit from grace.

"Sam," Frank said in an exhale. "I cheated on your mom. Twice." He had to get up and walk a little bit for this one. "I knew it was a mistake the first time. Then I did it again. I don't know. I guess I was lookin' for something."

"Did Mom ever know?"

"We didn't talk about it, but I knew she knew."

After a pause, Sam looked at his father. "We're quite the pair, aren't we?"

It was a strange time to do so. Totally inappropriate you could say. But at that moment, Frank Crawford started laughing, and Sam Crawford knew exactly where it was coming from. It was a "can't stop laughing, with tears rolling down" kind of laugh. Sam joined in. Their first laugh together in, well, forever.

It felt strange, but so life giving. Like sharing a delicious meal together for the first time. One that had a taste of letting go. And they both knew what it meant. It wasn't a making light of anything. It felt more like a coming home to their mutual humanity, by way of a path they both had been walking alone for so very long. A recognizing of how far they both had come, as they now met each other there. The laugh, an invitation to a future together that neither of them imagined.

When Sam caught his breath, it all turned on a dime. It started to settle in again just how long and how much he had ached for such a time as this. The tears this time showing him what they were holding and releasing. Telling him, *"Look out! Tsunami coming!"* Frank held his son until it passed.

"Oh my God," Frank said as they both got off the rollercoaster and collapsed on the couch. "What the hell just happened? Didn't see that coming. What are we, crazy?"

Sam shrugged. "I don't know. It just felt good. I'm going with that."

"Oh shit, son! Where do we go from here?"

All Sam could do was shake his head. "I have no idea. I guess we'll just have to take a step. Then another. One day at a time. Isn't that what they're telling you in AA these days?"

Frank shrugged. "Yeah."

And so that's what they did. The next step for Sam was sending his dad an email late that night. In it he talked about why his friend Tim told him he didn't judge him that day. How it resonated with him that the love everyone emerges from, and truly are, has no interest in or need to judge. That he had finally found it in himself. *Turns out,* he thought, *I did bring that color with me.*

He wrote of how he had come home to it, as he put it. He remembered how love's only interest is in what you've learned. How you've grown and healed. *Of course,* Sam thought, *what else would it care about?*

Frank would later send an email back, telling Sam he now knew what he was talking about. How his "higher power" and "The Power of Collective Powerlessness" group had greeted him with the same nonjudgment, and was now helping him off the insanity train.

In following emails they would both talk about what they've learned and grown into. They would ask each other questions they had long been wanting to ask. Each one ending with "Looking forward to being with you again."

The next time they saw each other in person at Finnegan's, it ended with that holy and beautiful three-word conversation they both had been seeking all along.

I love you, son. I love you, Dad.

Freeing and incredibly weird all at the same time. That's what it felt like. "Guess we'll get used to it," they'd both say.

Beauty that had been there all along. Colors waiting for their time.

4

12

The One About Wisdom

THE FOCUS OF THE NEXT WEEK'S SHOW was wisdom, and it couldn't have been better timing. Sam felt he had just experienced wisdom in Jadyn and Avery. And now, miracles of miracles, his dad. He felt a deep sense of knowing rising up within himself.

He thought back on the show a few weeks earlier about there always being a prior story, and how his viewers would have no idea what he'd lived through in recent days. But there he'd be, looking like the TV host everyone expected him to be.

The first guest was a philosophy professor at Newcastle University, and the other was a tavern owner. It had taken Sam about a week to convince Sol, the station's program manager, about the wisdom of inviting the second guest.

"Are you insane, Sam?"

"Let me explain, Sol. Sue Olsen owns Ole's Tavern back home. I met her through Tim, my first guest. I've spent lots of time talking with and observing her. She's amazing! She's one of the wisest people I've ever known. You get that way listening to and studying people at your tavern for thirty years. She's what you call 'street smart,' Sol."

"But we're just launching the show. It's way too early to take a risk like this, Sam!"

"Think about it. A prof and a tavern owner together. People will love the contrast. It's the Ivory Tower and the School of Hard Knocks. I'm telling you, people will love Sue! Would you at least FaceTime with her?

"Absolutely not! It's too risky!"

"Why do you only want to book *fancy* people with titles, and books they've written. Articles they've published. I detest the term, but why not have an average person on the show? Someone the average person can relate to?"

"No!"

An hour later Sol marched up to Sam's desk and said, "Okay. I'll FaceTime with her. Tomorrow morning."

The FaceTime Sol and Sue shared the next morning was epic. Everything that Sam hoped would happen did. Sue and Sol were both themselves. Afterward Sol marched over and planted his hands on Sam's desk. "Okay, Sam. The tavern lady's on, if she's game. I don't know. She thought it was crazy too."

It was then that Sol did something Sam had never seen him do. First he smiled, making Sam wonder what would happen to his face. Then he actually laughed. Out loud! "I love that woman!"

Sam called Sue immediately.

"Are you insane, Sam?"

"Why do people keep asking me that?" He then launched into all the reasons viewers would love her on the show.

"Look, I talked to your guy, but it all seems crazy to me. On TV?

"Sue, would you at least think about it, and get back to me soon?"

"Okay. I'll call ya later."

Soon came and went. No call from Sue. So he and Charlie RAV4 took the ninety-minute drive to Ole's Tavern. When Sue saw Sam walk in and take a seat in the booth under the old smoke eater, she came over, smiling and shaking her head the whole way. After she sat down, Sam simply looked her in the eyes. "Sue. Dear Sue. Please?"

"Sam Crawford! That ain't even fair! How can I say no now?"

And that is how you get a college professor and a tavern owner booked on the same show to talk about wisdom.

Carly: *And five, four, three . . .*

Sam: Good morning, and welcome to *You Are Love*. Our show is about *you*, really. We believe you *are* love. At your core. Your essence. When we think of love, we may think of being kind, or nice. But love is a host, a home, filled with wisdom. That will be our focus this morning.

I welcome our two guests today. Mary Roberts is chair of the philosophy department at Newcastle University. Professor Roberts also has a new book out, *The Philosophy of Wisdom*. Welcome, Professor Roberts. And welcome back, Shadow.

Shadow was in a different kind of mood this morning. Not her usual present self. She looked up at Sam. "Can we get on with it? I've got a lot of stuff to do today."

Mary: Good morning, Sam. I'm delighted to be here. Please, call me Mary.

Sam: I also welcome Sue Olsen. I came to know and admire Sue this past summer. She is the owner and head of the wisdom department at Ole's Tavern. Ole's is in Brayden, the town I lived and taught in for many years before coming to Newcastle.

Sue: Thank you for inviting me, Sam. Gotta admit I didn't see this one coming, but I appreciate being here.

Sam: *[laughing]* Well, here we are. Just your typical philosophy professor, tavern owner, and former high school physics teacher talking about wisdom on television.

The Heart of the Conversation

Sam: Mary, I appreciate how you start your book. Writing about where wisdom begins.

Mary: It begins where you would least expect it. Certainly not where the ego would tell you it comes from. Socrates in the fifth century BC said, "The only true wisdom is knowing you know nothing." Humility, he's saying, is what births true wisdom.

Sam: Sue?

Sue: Well, I've been observing folks in my tavern for thirty years. This Socrates guy had it right. The people in my tavern who think they know it all, don't know shit. Oh shit! I mean, sorry. Can I say that?

Sam gives her a smile and nods.

Anyway, the people in my tavern who think they know it all are pretending. One or two good questions about *how* they know what they claim to know, and their cover is blown.

Sam: As you can see, Sue's a pretty straight shooter.

Sue: It's the people who show some humility that I listen to and want to be around. It's interesting. The "know-it-alls" tend to sit together. I don't know why, cause it doesn't work. No one's listening. I guess they like to hear themselves talk.

Sam: I've been gifted in knowing another extremely wise woman, who has absolutely no reason for you to know she is. She knows that what she speaks of is infinitely greater than herself. She loves to say, "We don't know much."

Mary: Humility is *so* beautiful! It's the gateway. When we say we don't know, it opens us up to what life has to show and teach us. Science shows us the way with this. Science starts with humility and wonder. Nobody starts a laboratory because they know everything. Saying "I know" shuts us down. Closes us off.

Sue, you're showing a wisdom that comes from experience. Socrates also said that one of the three questions you should ask yourself before saying anything is, "Do I know that what I'm saying is true?" Oh, that we would all do that!

Sam: How can we know that *anything* is true?

Sue: My mother was one of the wisest people I ever knew. She'd often say to me, "You'll know it's true if it works." Does it play itself out in life to be true?

Mary: That's Eastern philosophy and spirituality right there, Sue!

Sue: I've also learned to trust my BS detector. It's reliable!

Sam: I can vouch for that! I saw you call people out so many times. Myself included.

After a while, like all the regulars, I learned to not even try with you!

Sue: Just give it to me straight. Just like life does.

Sam: Your wisdom comes from observing. Observing real life and how it works. Wisdom is knowing how the pieces fit and work together in life. That comes from experience.

Mary: That's how the Tao, the ancient Chinese philosophy, came to be. The Tao is attributed to Lao Tzu, who simply observed how life's nature, the Tao, is seen *in* nature. How it flowed and naturally brought about its beauty and truth. He wrote, "Life is a series of natural and spontaneous changes. Don't resist them. That only creates sorrow. Let reality be reality. Let things flow naturally forward in whatever way they like."

We're talking about what *life* wants. Not what the human ego wants, or thinks it needs.

Sue: Did you ever notice how people often say, "Things have a way of working out"? Whether they consider themselves "spiritual" or not? I see it all the time at my tavern in those people who get their heads out of their butts and pay attention. Get out of the way. Trust.

It's not that you don't *do* anything when you trust life. Seems to me you watch out for and cooperate with that flow thing you were talking about, Mary. The Tao. God.

Whatever you want to call it.

The ones who are fighting all the time. Fighting with life. Fighting with themselves and everybody around them. They make their own damn mess. It's like they're always swimming upstream.

Sam: Thank you, Sue. A friend, another Sue, told me of a haiku that I love. For those who may not know what a haiku is, it's a short poem that uses images from nature to speak of truth. This haiku says, "The fish swims upstream. The path of least resistance is too difficult." Often, the hardest and wisest thing is to not resist, and trust the flow.

Sue, you've spent decades observing people. What's the wisest thing to say about people, in general?

Sue: They need love.

Sam: That's it?

Sue: Yes.

Mary: I love your wisdom, Sue. You remind me of the Tao. Lao Tzu would say profound things in few words, such as, "Those who know do not speak. Those who speak do not know." There's a whole lot of truth in that to uncover, as you've already spoken of. We all probably know people who show us the truth of that.

Sue: Winnie the Pooh's my favorite philosopher. He says few words. Stuff like:

"Rivers know this: There is no hurry. We shall get there someday." I love that one.

"I must go forward where I have never been, instead of backwards where I have."

"When all else fails, take a nap." That one's served me well.

"People say nothing is impossible. But I do nothing every day."

When I'm tempted to make it too complicated, I remember Pooh.

Shadow looks up at Sam. "I like her."

Sam: I see Pooh in you, Sue! Who is your favorite philosopher, Mary?

Mary: Before this morning, I would have said Socrates. But it's now fast becoming Sue! Socrates doesn't have anything on you, my friend!

Sue: Socrates must have owned a tavern.

Mary: Socrates's core ideas were:

The importance of self-knowledge.

The unexamined life is not worth living.

The pursuit of virtue through knowledge.

He taught that there has to be a higher goal for all knowledge. And he loved the questioning process to uncover truth and understanding.

Sue: My best friend growing up was Jewish. When she'd come home from school, her mom would say, "Did you ask a good question today?" My parents would go straight to "What did you learn today? Tell me what you know."

Mary: Ah yes! The Jewish tradition, and Jewish philosophers, treasure the value of the questions themselves. First must always come the question, which comes from not knowing.

Sam: In a philosophy class in college, I came across the wisdom of Rainer Rilke, who wrote, "Be patient toward all that is unsolved in your heart, and to try to love the questions themselves . . . Do not now seek the answers, which cannot be given you, because you would not be able to live them. And the point is, to live everything. Live the questions now. Perhaps you will then gradually, without noticing it, live along some distant day into the answer."

Mary: That's beautiful. Everything in its own, wise time. Thank you, Rainer Rilke.

Sue: Having the humility and patience to let yourself live into the answers. That's what I've been trying to get my folks at the tavern to do, I guess.

Sam: Well, our time has gone by much too fast. Thank you, Mary Roberts. To our viewers, please read her beautiful book, *The Philosophy of Wisdom.*

And thank you, Sue Olsen. Viewers, if you're ever near Ole's Tavern in Brayden, there's always a welcome and some hard-earned wisdom waiting for you.

We'll be right back after this short break.

Carly: *And s.*

At the end of the show, Sam signs off.

Sam: Thank you for joining us this morning. Remember—"We're all just walking each other home," and you are love.

Carly: *And we're off.*

GUINNESS

13

Sam Crawford?

THE FOLLOWING WEEK SPED BY QUICKLY, as weeks often do. Thursdays were starting to feel like "Blursdays" to Sam. So at lunchtime on Fridays, Sam often walked over to Finnegan's for "Friday Fish and Chips." After days of prepping for Sunday's show, and learning more about the craft of television, it was comfort food, in what was fast becoming a comforting place. He sat on a stool at the bar on Fridays. In and out was the plan, and barstools seem to welcome anyone's agenda.

After ordering, Sam looked around the Daley—the large space off the bar where larger groups gathered, and live music is performed every Friday and Saturday night. A quartet of musicians was setting up for their weekend shows at the far end. One in particular caught his eye. The other eye too, actually. *Dang. She's gorgeous!* Sam thought as she started walking toward him.

"Sam Crawford?" she said, putting out her hand.

"Yeah!"

"Hi. I'm Maggie O'Brien. I've seen your show and really like it. So nice to meet ya."

"Nice to meet you too, Maggie, and thanks for watching. Looks like you're singing here this weekend."

"Yeah, the lads and I are here quite often. Love the crowds here. It's fun, and the free pints don't hurt either!"

Sam felt himself being drawn to her accent, and then asked, "You sing other places, too?"

"Yeah." She winked. "We make the rounds at only the finest establishments. You free tonight? Stop by and give it a listen."

Sam thought of the night he had planned with Shadow. *Sorry, girl. Got other plans.*

"I am. I'd love to come."

"We start at eight. Grand to meet ya, Sam!"

"Grand to meet you, Maggie!"

Grand? You said grand? he thought to himself, turning to the bar as she walked away. *You never say grand. Tryin' too hard, Crawford!*

And so it was. A TV guy finished his fish and chips, and walked back to the station with a smile and a spring in his step.

At his first meeting after lunch, the big guy's mind kept leaving the room. *C'mon, Crawford. Close the mechanism.* Yes, it does work about 90 percent of the time. Maggie O'Brien was clearly in the 10 percent.

He just happened to arrive at Finnegan's well before eight. Perhaps the luck of the Irish left a small table open in front of the stage.

"Dia daoibh! And good evening! How are ye?" Maggie said as the band took the stage to a raucous crowd. Many of which were clearly groupies.

Maggie looked at Sam. "Welcome, Sam! Grand ya came!" she said as Sam lifted his pint.

The Irish Way, as they were called, began with "Finnegan's Wake."

Tim Finnegan lived in Walkin Street
A gentle Irishman, mighty odd
He'd a beautiful brogue so rich and sweet
And to rise in the world he carried a hod
You see he'd a sort of the tipp' lin' way
With the love of the liquor, poor Tim was born
And to help him on with his work each day
He'd a drop of the craythur every morn.

The crowd was yelling and lifting their pints. Sam Crawford never felt so Irish.

"And now," Maggie announced after taking a sip. "A tribute to that wonderful Dublin fishmonger, who may have been selling a wee bit more than her cockles and mussels. Molly Malone!"

"Take us to Dublin, Maggie!" someone yelled from the back.

In Dublin's fair city
Where the girls are so pretty
I first set me eyes on sweet Molly Malone
As she wheeled her wheelbarrow
Through the streets, broad and narrow,
Crying, "Cockles and mussels, alive, alive, oh"

The crowd shouted the refrain:

Alive, alive, oh
Alive, alive, oh
Crying, "Cockles and mussels, alive, alive, oh"

Four more songs followed, ending with what was a surprise to Sam, but clearly not to the crowd. Maggie did a magic trick. As was her custom, she performed a card trick, much to the crowd's delight. Especially the volunteer. One Sam Crawford.

After she amazed everyone, Maggie shouted, "We'll be back in fifteen! Toast the night!"

"Thanks for playing along, Sam. Good fun!" she said as she joined Sam at his table.

"Whoa. You're really good, Maggie!"

She laughed. "I work part time at Shenanigan's Magic Shop on the west side. I've always loved magic and illusions."

"How did you do that?"

Maggie's magical wink told him, "Maybe someday I'll tell ya."

Sam laughed. "And your group?"

"Been playin' together for ten years now. We have a good time together. Good musicians. Good lads."

"You can tell how much you like each other. You sound great!"

"Thank ya. So, Sam. I really *do* like your show. I'm probably like most everyone who watches it. I need it these days. Lots goin' on."

Studying Sam for a moment, she leaned forward. "Ya look like ya've got some hard-won wisdom in ya. Like ya've been through some cac."

"Some what?"

"Irish word for shit."

"Yeah. Cac. To be sure."

"I guess we all have."

"Sam, you stickin' round for the second set?"

Sam lifted his pint.

"Grand! You see that old gentleman over there? Name is Angus. Angus McGee. Do yourself a favor and get to know him sometime. I'm going to go say hello. See ya later."

After the break, the second set began with "Star of the County Down."

Near Banbridge town, in the County Down
One morning in July
Down a boreen green came a sweet colleen
And she smiled as she passed me by

She looked so sweet from her two bare feet
To the sheen of her nut-brown hair.
Such a coaxing elf, I'd like to shook myself
For to see I was really there.

The crowd sang and lifted their pints at the chorus:

From Bantry Bay down to Derry Quay
And from Galway to Dublin town
No maid I've seen like the brown colleen
That I met in the County Down

The show ended with the Irish Way's traditional, "The Parting Glass," to which the crowd stood in reverence.

Of all the money that e'er I had
I spent it in good company
and of all the harm that e'er I did,
alas it was to none but me

And all I've done for want of wit
To memory now I can't recall
So, fill to me the parting glass
Good night and joy be with you all.

"You've been such good company! Good night to ye!" Maggie shouted as the band played on.

As the band was taking down their set, Sam asked if they'd be willing to be on the show in a month. The "lads" looked at each other, as if they'd just been asked if they loved the motherland, and the deal was done. He asked Maggie if he could help carry anything out.

"How sweet of ya, Sam, to invite us! Sure! If ya'd be so kind to take those two mic stands."

As they walked out, Maggie realized Sam had always been sitting when they chatted. The height difference was nothing new for Sam. But for one Maggie O'Brien, at 5'5", standing next to a guy 6'8" was a relatively new experience.

"You're a tall drink of water, Sam Crawford!"

"Yeah, been this way for a while now."

Sam watched them put everything in their van. *Everything* had its one true home.

"Looks like you've all done this before."

Someone from the band nodded. "That we have."

Maggie walked up to Sam, paused a moment, and said, "I mentioned before that it looks like ya've been through some things. I've been too, for some time now." Looking up as if she was checking out what was inside that face and heart way above her, she said, "I've got a feelin' we've some things to talk about, ya and me. Ever been up to the lookout, on top of the bluff on Wicklow Road? It's beautiful up there at night. My favorite spot."

"No. I keep hearing about it."

"How bout I pick ya up, and we go up there sometime?"

"Sure." Sam nodded, trying not to look too pathetic.

"How 'bout Monday night?"

"Perfect!"

14

Maggie's Bluff

THE YELLOW VW VAN PULLED UP to his house. Sam and Shadow had been looking out the window for fifteen minutes. Shadow had no idea what she was looking for, but she knew Sam thought it to be most important. Sam wasn't sure either. All he knew was how much he wanted to find out.

Maggie O'Brien got out of her van wearing black jeans and a light green sweater with a dark brown scarf that made her auburn hair the most beautiful thing Sam had seen in a very long time. While most of her colors played right into Shadow's color blindness, she looked at Sam with a look of *I like her!* Shadow ran to the door and barked at Maggie's knock.

"Hi, Maggie!" Sam said, as Shadow began showing her just how much she *did* like her.

"Sorry, this is Shadow. She's really a sweetheart. Just wanted you to feel welcome."

"Oh, dear Shadow," Maggie said as she got down on her knees. "So nice to meet ya! Oh, you *are* a dear!

"I love dogs! Especially goldens!" Maggie said, looking up at Sam.

Shadow turned to Sam, then back to Maggie, letting her know again in no uncertain terms how she felt about her. "Oh, Shadow. Sam? How about she comes along?"

"Hear that? You're in, girl!" Making the move that always told Shadow it's a wonderful world, he grabbed her lifeline to everything she loved. Her leash.

"Thanks for inviting us, Maggie." Sam smiled, as the threesome piled into the van.

"You're gonna love it up there, Sam. Shadow will too."

"Do you live here in town?"

"On the west side. A few blocks from Shenanigan's Magic Shop."

"How long?"

"I came here with my parents when I was thirteen. We're from Howth, a town near Dublin. My parents live four blocks from me. We get back to Ireland once a year or so. My brother lives in Malehide. Our family's pretty close. Ya probably haven't been here too long, Sam, what with the show so new."

"No. A few months now."

When they arrived at the top of the bluff, Maggie got two camping chairs out from the back of her van, and grabbed her thermos.

"Over there, right between those two trees. *That's* my spot!"

When they settled in, Shadow looked down on the city. *Yup. I knew I'd like this!*

The smells were unbelievable up there. They seemed to be coming from everywhere. She ran from tree to bush, while always staying in sight of Sam. Eventually she settled down at Sam's feet, being sure to face this one who answered to the sound of "Maggie."

After sitting down, Sam took it all in. Newcastle's lights were surrounded by those comforting bluffs, now turning darker shades of gray. "This *is* beautiful. I can see why you love coming here."

"Ah, yes. It reminds me of when my family would take the cliff walk to Howth Head. There's great views of Dublin Bay and Lambay Island there. We'd picnic up there. Play music."

"You come from a family of musicians?"

"Yeah, Mum plays the fiddle and Irish harp. My father, the accordion and banjo. My brother, Shawn, got pretty good on the Irish flute and fiddle. I've pretty much stuck with the fiddle, guitar, tin whistle, and concertina. I'm a fortunate one. My parents are awesome. Gave me a foundation that I'm standing on today. We all need that, to be sure," she said, turning to Sam.

"How'd they do that?"

"Lovin' me. Lookin' back, I don't remember them sayin' much to me about life, or how to live it. They just lived what they were. What they believed in ... faith. They were strong Irish Catholics. We went to church often. I didn't think much of it at the time, but I remember feeling so safe there. The people were lovely.

"They lived family. I saw its value. Treating people the right way was everything to them. My people are kind, gentle, hard workin'. Been through a lot. It was the community pulling together that got them through. I think that's why they value being kind and respectful. They knew they needed each other. It was just the way of things there.

"Here," she said, opening up the thermos. "Want some hot tea?"

Raising their two mugs, they toasted. "To kindness!"

A long pause followed. Long enough for Sam to notice how remarkably comfortable the silence felt with this one from Howth that he'd just met.

The Heart of the Conversation

"So tell me about you, Maggie O'Brien. Anything," the tall guy said, as they looked out over the city's lights.

"Oh my. Where to start?" she said.

Sam turned to her. "What makes you happy?"

"Connection," she quickly said. "People together. Singin'. Laughin'. Liftin' each other up. Music ... I love magic," she said, looking up at the stars. "Finding the magic in life. What there are no words for, but shows ya the wonder of it all. How about *ya,* Sam?"

"This," the big guy said as he looked around. "Everything this is."

Feeling no need to speak, they sat. Accompanied by the satisfaction in Shadow's long, deep breath and exhale.

Maggie broke the silence. "What'd ya do before comin' to Newcastle?"

"I taught high school physics for twenty years. The station manager's an old friend from college. Heather, for some reason, believed I could do it. Got me to start believing it myself."

"That was quite a leap for ya to take from being a teacher to hosting your own TV show. Gotta say, ya look like a natural, Sam. Like this is the natural next step for ya."

"Well, as I said on the first show, I'd been through some things. Some cac, as you say," Sam said, looking out over the city as if it was his life. "And was starting to come out the other side of it all, when Heather shared KLUV's vision with me. I thought we'd be a good fit for each other. A chance to share with a larger audience the kinds of things that had gotten me through, and were giving me new life. To keep learning from my guests intrigued me.

"And . . ." He was looking over the city. "It was time to move on. Turn the page. Next chapter."

"Yeah. I know about that," Maggie said, turning to Sam.

Sam noticed the joy and hope her words gave him. He turned toward her. It was the first time Sam had really taken in her beautiful green eyes, the likes of which he'd never seen.

He sensed that fierce, independent spirit within her that he'd felt at Finnegan's. The same he had known in Jadyn.

"Movin' on," she said, looking down at the town. "Can ya imagine the stories down there, Sam. The stories of the past. The stories being lived, and the ones on their way."

With their gaze still on the lights below, Maggie broke the silence again. "My husband, Caleb, died two years ago."

"Oh, Maggie. I'm so sorry."

"Thank ya. You're very kind. Cancer. Stomach cancer. It spread . . . he was a fireman. Later a fire inspector. It happens to those in that kind of work. We were together fourteen years. Married, twelve."

Sam looked over at her, waiting to see what the moment called for. Taking its cue, he turned his chair toward her, sat down, and leaned toward those green eyes that held so much. "What was that like for you?"

"Hell. One day he's the healthiest, strongest fella ya ever could know. Then it started showin' up. The coughin'. Shortness of breath. Stomach pain. He wasn't much for going to doctors, but when he finally did, they gave him six months. He made it nine . . . should have pressed him more to go earlier to the doctor, I guess. I still beat myself up over that. Maybe it would have . . . I don't know. Just watching him deteriorate. A little less of him every day. I felt like a little girl watching the air slowly goin' out of her only balloon she'd been holdin' for a long time."

Sam leaned forward. "Tell me about him."

Green eyes filling with tears are a most powerful thing. "Sorry. It still just comes out."

"Of course it does."

She half smiled. "I don't know. Maybe it helps to be Irish at a time like that. We Irish are good with the sad. It's home for us in a lot of ways."

Looking out at the city, she continued, "Caleb was a renaissance man. Wasn't much he wasn't interested in. Wasn't much he couldn't do. Could talk to anyone about anything. His greatest love was his family. They were everything to him. What I first loved about him. We Irish are a family-centered people."

Turning to Sam with a look of amazement still very much alive, she leaned back in her chair, looking up at the stars. "He loved makin', buildin', fixin' things. If he didn't know how, he just figured it out. He was a good musician too. Guitar. Banjo. Harmonica. I taught him some fiddle. He wrote some lovely songs. He was totally into art his last years. Painting. Loved going to art museums."

"How did you meet?"

"He came into Shenanigan's one day. Said he wanted to start learnin' magic.

"Huh," she said, nodding her head. "Turned out, we found it in each other."

Sam returned his gaze to the city. "You're right, Maggie. Think of the stories down there. Watching you at Finnegan's Friday night, you'd never know yours."

"We all put on a show, Sam Crawford."

Sam nodded, looking like he was watching a few of his own. "Yes we do," he said in the silence. "Yes we do."

He drifted away to all the times he sat in his car in the school parking lot on mornings during his separation and divorce. Trying to get himself to go inside and put on the show. The one where he's that teacher everyone knew. Confident. In charge. Bigger than life. People had been looking up to him forever, it seemed.

"Sometimes I feel like I'm looking down on it all these days," she said, looking at the city. "Watching someone *else's* life. Then I have to go back down, and be in it all."

Shadow never took her gaze off Maggie. She was listening her way into a sacred space that only a dog and a remarkable woman can know.

"The music's pure therapy these days, Sam. When the crowd is joinin' in, singin' and clappin', I feel a little like I'm back with family again. But it's not the same. Someone's missin' in the crowd."

Shadow walked over to Maggie's hand on the arm of her chair, licked it, and gave her oxytocin therapy. Maggie leaned down to gently stroke the back of her new friend who seemed to know her like an old friend. "Ah, you sweet lady. I'm sorry, Sam. Look at me. Goin' on here. I want to know about you. Ya have kids?"

Sam spent the next twenty minutes talking about Avery, all an extra chromosome twenty-one can bring into a life, and Ben.

"Do you have kids?" Sam asked.

"I miscarried three times. I knew after the second one, I only had one more try left in me. One percent of women have three or more," she sighed. "Guess there can't be a one percent without someone in it. It was hard for us. Reminders every day. Just seein' kids out and about. Bein' round friends with kids. Knowin' our friends were feelin' awkward talkin' about their kids around us. Growing up in my family, I desperately wanted to be a mum. Caleb would have been a grand dad to be sure. Hard to make sense of it, really. We, of course, thought about adopting. But, I don't know. Never worked out."

"Oh, Maggie. I can't imagine how hard that was for you both."

"Over time, I began to accept that maybe I was supposed to have children in my life in other ways. I started working part time at a day care and preschool near our house. I'm still there, and love it. And I love visiting my niece and nephew in Ireland. FaceTiming with them. It fills the void. Partly."

"Those kids need you."

The conversation danced its way into lots of other things that night, while lifting another mug of her special brew of hot tea.

Before this evening, the thought of meeting someone and starting all over felt overwhelming to Sam. Sometimes questioning if he would ever have the energy to start over again with someone. But this wasn't feeling like that at all. No. Not this night.

Sam told Maggie that he loved her accent. He'd notice it when she said things like, "That was foon!" Or, "So loovely." She laughed. "What accent? *You're* the one with the accent! Been here almost thirty years now, but I've hung on to it a bit. It's who and what I am, Sam. I'm proud of it. Proud of my heritage. My people. My ancestors who did the hard thing of coming here and settlin'."

"I think it's beautiful, Maggie." *And so are you,* he thought, but stopped short of saying it.

Sam asked questions about growing up in Ireland, and about her brother. Maggie gladly regaled him with stories of her family and Irish culture.

Sam told her more of what it was like growing up in his family. His father. His basketball and teaching days. Much more than he ever thought he would.

He talked about his divorce, but didn't mention the reason it ended, and the pain he'd caused. Maggie sensed he was holding a secret. Magicians know these things. She never asked.

In the quiet of early morning, the three pulled up at Sam's house. Sam was searching for how he wanted the night to end. He had to let her know how much this time had meant to him. But what would be right?

As they talked in her van a little more, Sam decided it safe to kiss her on the cheek. As he moved toward her, Maggie stopped him. Sudden confusion and regret came over him that he'd done something wrong. Reaching out her hands, she placed them on either side of

Sam's face. Holding him there, the wisdom in the green eyes showed Sam the way. She kissed him. A kiss that Sam wondered if he would ever know again. One that surprised him, but felt so right. They sat looking at each other, taking in what was happening.

"Maggie, I want to see—"

She kissed him a second time.

"Me too, Sam."

As he was getting out of the car, he heard, "Sam?"

"Yes?"

She just shook her head. "Never mind. Thanks for a lovely night."

Sam and his Shadow went straight to the den and started a fire. In its light he looked around, and in the bookshelves imagined once again that library of his life. The one that held his stories.

Remembering Maggie's words that night as they looked down on Newcastle. "Can ya imagine the stories down there, Sam? The stories on their way?"

Looking into the fire, he smiled, as if he had picked up a new arrival off the shelf, and was reading its first line. "I love finding the magic in life."

15

The One About Grief

SAM SPENT THE NEXT WEEKS aware of her presence. Looking through eyes that suddenly saw a world that had been there all along, but was now suddenly full of magic. Colors seemed brighter. The air crisp and invigorating. Food had more taste, it seemed.

He noticed, for the first time, a large mural on his walk from his home to the station. A mural depicting the arrival of the earliest Irish settlers coming off their ship. Their bodies weary. Their eyes searching for anything telling them they made the right decision. Their children's eyes full of wonder. *Has that mural always been there?*

People seemed to be greeting him with a smile. Much more than usual. Curious as to why, it finally dawned on him that he had been doing the same.

The week arrived for the Irish Way to be on the show. He had invited three guests to be in the episode. The first was Carol Finnegan, the mom of his best friend, Charlie. For her own healing, she had dedicated much of her time working with other moms who suddenly lost a child. When Sam called to invite her to tell her story, she leapt at the chance to be of help to a larger audience.

The second guest was a Newcastle resident, Joan Safford. Sam had visited her following a conversation he had with one of the crew, who knew of her experience in caring for her husband through his three-year battle with ALS. He had heard her speak at the community center.

The third guest would be Kelly Andrews, a local medium. Both Carol and Joan had agreed to have a reading with her on the show. It was a risk for KLUV, but surprisingly, Sol signed off.

With Carly's five-finger flash and finger point, it was showtime.

Sam: Good morning, thank you so much for joining us again on *You Are Love*. I'm your host, Sam Crawford. We have an inspiring show this morning. One that will touch your heart, I'm sure. Our guest segment will focus on grief, loss, and newfound purpose.

We'll close out the show with a wonderful band called the Irish Way. They've gained quite a following over the years.

For those of you who are here for the first time, this is Shadow. Thanks for being with us, girl. For helping us through, just by being.

It's my honor to introduce you to our guests, Carol Finnegan and Joan Safford.

Welcome.

Carol is no stranger to me, to say the least. She was my second mom growing up. Mother of my best friend, Charlie.

Carol: And you, my dear Sam, are my second son. Always will be. A dear friend to Charlie. So grateful for you.

Sam: Carol, would you tell Charlie's story to our audience?

Carol: My son had just graduated from high school, along with Sam. Charlie and Sam had been inseparable since the second grade. On this day they were driving separate cars to our community center to play basketball. Charlie was a few minutes ahead of Sam. Charlie was hit on the driver's side at high speed by a distracted driver who ran a red light. He was brought to the hospital, but his heart stopped in the ambulance. They revived him, but he died in the emergency room.

Sam: A day that changed both our lives forever. I came on the scene a few minutes after the crash. I knew right away it was him, and I knew it was bad. I was just hysterical. All I remember is yelling at the police officer to let me get to the car.

Carol: The accident happened three blocks from our house. The police came to our door. I don't remember much of anything the officer said. The next thing I do remember is being at the hospital. Sam, you were there.

Sam: It was so chaotic. *What just happened?* You try and take it in, but you just can't.

Carol: I certainly couldn't. Thank you for crying with me, Sam.

Sam reached out and put his hand on Carol's. He took a Coach Ferguson breath.

Sam: Joan Safford, your story of loss and grief is different, as they all are.

Joan: Yes. My husband, John, lived with ALS for three years. He transitioned, died, two years ago.

Sam: So for you, Joan, a long, gradual process of losing a spouse. For you, Carol, a sudden, completely unexpected loss.

Carol: Yes. I now meet with moms primarily who have experienced sudden death. It has its own trauma. You're suddenly thrust into such shock. Confusion.

Sam: Carol, how did you come to be involved with parents who have suffered a sudden loss?

Carol: About two years after Charlie was killed, I wanted to help parents who were going through what I did. It's amazing how you want to run right to the pain you share with someone else. And I knew it would help me in my own healing. I connected with Parents Touch, a nonprofit in our community that provides support for parents who have experienced the loss of a child. You feel so alone. Friends, even family, often don't know how to respond to you.

Sam: Help us understand that deep connection.

Carol: People use the term "street cred." I've got "mom cred." People I meet with know that I know what it feels like. I mostly listen. Hold a hand. Cry with. Give a hug.

Sam: I notice you're not talking about what you *say* to them.

Carol: No. Speaking to them is not the first place I go. And I only talk about my own feelings and experience when I see that it could be helpful. I focus on asking questions, providing space for them to tell the story of their child.

Sam: Do you give *any* advice?

Carol: Only when I know enough to be reasonably sure it could help. You know, we're a hard bunch to talk to—parents who have lost a child. Rarely do words help us. I've had well-meaning people tell me so many unhelpful things. Things that make you just want to scream at the person.

Sam: Could you give an example?

Carol: For me, the ones that bothered me the most were the comments that involved God in some way. "He's in a better place." "God wanted him in heaven." "You'll see him again in heaven." Those kinds of things.

I just wanted to scream, "A better place is here!" "I want him here! With me!" Or, "Why are you telling me to hate God? The one who took my child away from me? I'm supposed to find comfort in *that*?" That's how I honestly felt when I heard those words.

Sam: People *do* want to help in some way. What do you suggest?

Carol: As far as what to *say*—don't! Don't say anything except "I'm sorry." Don't try and make me feel better. I didn't want to feel better for quite a while. I needed people to accept me as I was. It was my only connection. I knew I had to find my own way.

And it changed not only day to day, but moment to moment. I never knew what would trigger me, or when. It would come from things you wouldn't expect. So just ask, "How is it today?"

As far as what to *do*... just be. Show up. Call. Listen. And be in it for the long haul.

People tend to drift off, stay away because *they're* uncomfortable, or think you should be getting better when *they* think you should. There is no statute of limitations. And what is *"better"* anyway?

Sam: Thank you, Carol. No, there is no statute. I'm still grieving Charlie. To this day something will happen and I think, "Gotta tell Charlie about that. He'll love it!" And then the sadness pays a visit. Again.

Carol: Me too.

Sam: Joan, tell us the story of your dear husband, John.

Joan: When dying is a longer process, you know a series of griefs. One week, as I'm watching John lose his ability to walk, I'd think of all our walks together. The runs we went on. We were both avid runners. I grieved all of that leaving us.

Another time, I'm watching him lose his ability to swallow. I'd grieve the loss of all the meals we shared. John loved to cook. Grill, especially. I loved baking. I would grieve sitting down together for a meal at home. The great conversations at the table.

We had our favorite restaurants that we loved to visit. We'd reserve our own special table at a few of them. It's a slow letting go. One that never seems to end.

Sam: What was it like when the end finally *did* come?

Joan: I was so exhausted by that time. Numb. I even felt a little guilty. Guilty over the relief I felt. Guilty over not feeling enough of the sadness I thought I *should* be feeling.

I was a zombie at his service. It was all a blur.

The grief of him not being in the house didn't really start until I felt the silence. It was so painfully quiet. John loved to talk with people, but he couldn't say much toward the end. So I'd do the talking. He'd nod slightly. Just knowing he was still there, still in that body, helped.

Sam: For a long-term caregiver, such as yourself, what was helpful from other people?

Joan: Breaks. People who would offer to come over and sit with John so I could leave the house. Shop. Run errands. Go have coffee with a friend. Take a walk. A nap.

For me, it was the same as Carol. I didn't need people to say anything. Didn't want people to try and make me feel better. They couldn't. Like Carol said, just be. With me.

For me. For us.

Sam: And what is helpful now?

Joan: I need people who won't forget. Forget me or John. That friend who will call just to check in. I'm talking for the long haul. I certainly haven't forgotten. Anything!

I love it when someone will take me out for coffee. Tell John stories. Please don't be afraid to talk about him. I need that. It helps.

Sam: Carol?

Carol: Thank you, Joan. Me too. We often think it's too painful for someone to talk about the one they've lost. But it's just the opposite. Or, just talk about other things. Laugh. I'm still alive and in the world. I still have a life. I often say, "I'm not the same, but I'm still me."

As you mentioned, people drop off after a while. They think you're probably over the hard part. I've found that many of us appreciate someone taking the initiative to make contact.

Joan: I've learned that *I* need to take the initiative, when I'm able. Not just wait for someone to contact me. It's helped me to say, "Hi. I need to talk. Now."

Not everyone has those people in their lives. My heart goes out to them. But it only takes one or two.

Sam: Our conversation now reminds me of the quote from spiritual teacher Ram Dass. I always refer to it at the end of each show. "We're all just walking each other home." It applies to grief, too. What would "home" look like for the two of you in terms of your grief?

Carol: Space to be authentic. Space to remember however I want to remember that day. Some kind of peace.

Joan: Yes, and I'd find a home in anyone who will accept me as I am. Whatever I'm feeling on any given day. A place in them where there is a welcome room for my questions, anger, sadness. Someone who will listen to the stories of my heart. Even five, ten years down the road. *[Joan looks at Shadow.]* Just like this dear soul.

Sam: Joan, you used the word "transition" to describe John's passing.

Joan: John and I were part of the Unity church for thirty years here in Newcastle. I still am. We speak of death as transition. Reminding ourselves that it is only the body that dies. The soul merely transitions to a different state of being. The soul is eternal.

Sam: Well, with that in mind, after this commercial break, Carol and Joan have both agreed to meet with a local medium. To see if they can hear from Charlie and John. We'll be right back.

Commercial Break

Carly: *Five, four, three, two, one . . .*

Sam: And we're back. I'm here with Carol Finnegan, who suddenly lost her eighteen-year-old son, Charlie, in a car accident. And Joan Safford, whose husband died from ALS after a three-year battle.

Now, I'd like to introduce you to our third guest, Kelly Andrews. Kelly is a medium and lives here in Newcastle. She specializes in communicating with loved ones on the other side, and channeling their messages to their loved ones here.

Our guests have both agreed to have a reading with Kelly. Carol, you've never done anything like this before?

Carol: No, I haven't. But I've learned to open myself up to anything that feels right to try. This feels "right," for some reason.

Sam: Thank you, Carol, for your openness. Especially for doing this for the first time on television.

Kelly, could you tell us a little about yourself and what you do?

Kelly: For me, growing up, I saw deceased people. They'd talk with me. It all just seemed normal to me. When I realized no one else was experiencing what I was, I kept it to myself until my husband died. I struggled with any connection with him. Maybe it was because my grief was so intense he couldn't get through to me. So I went to a medium a friend recommended. A neutral party, so to speak.

I found it so helpful. I wanted to help others as I had been helped. I've been practicing mediumship for twenty-two years now. I've met with around four thousand clients.

Sam: Thank you. You ready, Carol?

Carol: I am! Nervous, though.

Sam: Joan?

Joan: I've always been curious about this. Sure!

Kelly: I understand. Perfectly normal. I want you to know that I've been in contact with Charlie and John several times this week. This morning they've both been particularly chatty. Especially during the show now. They have a lot to say about what you've been talking about.

Give me a moment here . . . "This is Charlie." Oh, sweet! This is something he's showing me so you know it's really him. Deceased loved ones will often do that. They know it's hard for us here, and we need assurance. He's making a heart shape with his hands, and pulsing it toward his chest.

Carol: Oh my! *[Tears begin welling up.]* I did that with Charlie when he was little, putting him to bed. It was our little signal that I was with him through the night.

Kelly: He's saying, "I've been with you. Always. I was with you in the waiting room at the hospital. Trying to let you know I was okay." Now he's showing me some red shoes. Does that make any sense?

Sam: Oh my God! The chaplain was wearing red shoes! I remember them because it seemed so weird.

Kelly: He's saying, "I was trying so hard to let you know I was alright."

Now he's showing me a picture . . . and kissing it. He's saying, "Mom, I've loved it when you kiss my picture."

Carol: *[Takes a deep breath.]* For years I've kissed his picture before I go to bed.

Kelly: Wait . . . oh. He's saying he's so proud of you and how you're helping others in their grieving.

Now he's holding up his finger, saying he has one more thing to say! He loves it when you go to the cemetery. He knows you need to do that. He smiles when you bring things for him. He's showing me a tiny . . . ball. Orange?

Carol: Oh my. I've brought several little basketballs to his grave.

Kelly: But he wants you to know that he's with you . . . "any and everywhere" he says. "Just keep talking to me like you always did . . . because I'm still with you. Always."

Carol: This is amazing! I've been talking to him. Hoping he could somehow hear me. Now I know! Thank you, Charlie. I will. I love you so much!

Kelly: "Love you too, Mama!"

Carol: Mama! That's what he called me when he was little.

Kelly: . . . Okay. And John's been waiting patiently, Joan. He's telling me he loves it when you and your . . . two girls get together on Sunday evenings for dinner. He's often there . . . loves it when you share stories. Family trips. He shows me an island . . . *F* . . . starts with an *F*.

Joan: Fiji. We loved it there.

Kelly: Did you go on . . . like a . . . gondola ride there, or something? . . . Now I'm seeing it stop moving.

Joan: Yes! The four of us were stuck up there for four hours. Oh my God!

Kelly: . . . Now he's showing me a classroom . . . and saying, "Everything is a school. Life on earth is an Earth School for the soul. We're here to learn . . . to grow.

"If we choose to use it in that way. I was there to learn patience . . . letting go . . . trusting. To not try and control everything."

Joan: I saw his struggle with that every day. I sure did.

Kelly: I can't tell you all how many times I've heard the message from the other side that life is a school for the soul. I hear it over and over.

Oh! John says he's going to go for a run now, but wants you to know, Joan, how grateful he was to share in this life and love with you.

Joan puts her face in her hands and Shadow puts her head on her lap.

Okay, now . . . Charlie's got something for *you*, Sam . . . He's showing me this big box. He's holding it up . . . he's saying there's so much in it. He wants to show you what's in there. But at another time. "Just the two of us," he says. And, he points to me. "The three of us," he's saying.

Sam: You're on, Charlie!

Carol, Joan, and Kelly, I can't thank you enough for sharing this profound and incredible time with me and our viewers this morning.

Stay with us. We'll be right back with the Irish Way.

Carly: *And we're off.*

Commercial Break

During the commercial break, Sam chatted with Joan and Carol. He gave Maggie a hug while the band was getting in place.

Carly: *And five, four, three, two, one . . .*

Sam: Welcome back. If you've been to Finnegan's Pub here in Newcastle, you may have heard this amazing band, the Irish Way. Thank you for being with us this morning.

Maggie: Thank you for inviting us, and we would like to offer a heartfelt thanks to Carol and Joan for being so vulnerable with us all this morning. In honor of Charlie Finnegan and John Safford, we'd like to sing a song we end all of our shows with. A traditional Irish song, "The Parting Glass."

Of all the money ere I had,
I spent it in good company,
And all the harm I've ever done,
Alas it was to none but me.

And all I've done for want of wit,
To memory now I can't recall.
So, fill to me the parting glass,
Goodnight and joy be with you all.

Of all the comrades that e'er I had
They're sorry for my going away
And all the sweethearts that e'er I had
They would wish me one more day to stay

But since it fell into my lot
That I should rise and you should not
I'll gently rise and softly call
Good night and joy be to you all

So fill to me the parting glass,
And drink a health whate'er befalls
Then gently rise and softly call
Good night and joy be to you all

Good night and joy be to you all.

Sam: The Irish Way! Thank you so much. Stop by Finnegan's Pub for some more music!

And to our viewers, a deep thanks for being with us today. We'll see you next Sunday, when my guest will be political commentator Elizabeth Sheldon.

Remember, "we're all just walking each other home." You are love.

Carly: *And we're off.*

Maggie immediately ran up to Sam when they were off the air, wrapping her arms around him. "Oh, Sam. I'm so sorry ya lost your best friend so tragically. So young."

"Thanks. I was surprised by how good it was to talk about him again. Especially with Charlie's mom."

"Do ya think you're going to go see Kelly?"

"Yeah. I do. I want to do it for Charlie."

"I was so touched by the connections you all had. Would ya be okay if I went with ya, Sam? I think I want to try and connect with Caleb! Would that be too uncomfortable for ya? I'd understand. The whole thing's a might weird, I guess."

"I think I'd like to have you with me, when it's just me and Charlie. And I understand your wanting to hear from Caleb. Sure. Let's do it! We can be there for each other."

12

16

The Big Guy Tries a Medium

ON THE DRIVE OVER TO Kelly Andrew's house later that week, Sam began to have second thoughts. *What if Caleb does show up? Do I really want to be around that? Crawford, get out of yourself! If you care for her, you'd be happy for her.*

When he pulled up to Kelly's house, it calmed him to see Maggie's van waiting. The thought came, *It's good we're here for each other. Just go with it.*

When Maggie came out of her van, she took in the house where she would hopefully do something she hadn't done for two years. Speak with her husband.

"I've been connecting with both Charlie and Caleb this morning," Kelly told them as she walked them to her meeting room in the back of the house. "They're both excited. Very eager to do this. They have a lot they want to say."

Sam and Maggie looked at each other. *We're really doing this!*

They sat in two chairs close to each other, facing Kelly, and looked around. They saw the crystals and the wall hanging that said, "Karma's a Bitch," and smelled burnt sage.

Kelly looked over at Sam. "You look nervous."

"Yeah, I am. Mostly anxious to see what happens. To be honest, I want this to be real, but part of me is still skeptical. Even after everything that happened on the show. Is that weird?"

"That's all normal, Sam. Just pay attention to what's going on in here," Kelly said, pointing to her gut. "Is it ringing true for you? Is it feeling authentic? Maggie, do you have any questions?"

"No. Gotta say, though, that a couple of weeks ago it wasn't exactly on my radar to be here. But life's magical. I love that about life." She looked around the room, and took a deep breath. "Sitting here now, I'm anticipating the magic."

"Magic! Yes, this is magical you could say. But it's also real. No tricks here. No illusions. It's actually normal," Kelly said, "at least in my world!

"Alright, give me a moment here."

A long silence followed. Sam and Maggie didn't know what to do. *Should we look at Kelly? Leave her alone? Look around the room?*

Kelly looked over to her left, and shook her head. "Okay . . . Charlie, you're really talking fast. Could you slow down a little?"

Sam started having the same thoughts he was having on the show. *This seems real. Charlie always talked so fast. Like he had a lot to say that needed to get out. Even if he was the only one who thought so.*

"Alright . . . He's got that box with him. He pulls out this old newsboy-style hat, puts it on, and is kind of doing a little swagger thing, like he thinks he's pretty cool."

Okay, Sam thought. *Can't google that!*

"Yeah. Charlie loved that kind of hat. He was the only kid who would wear one. Old guys wear those, I kept telling him. He thought it made him look mature. Wise. I told him you're gonna need a lot more than a hat for that!"

"Now he's taking out a basketball, and spinning it on his finger. Big smile." Kelly looked confused. "He's running around a little, like he's following someone. Does that make sense?"

"Right behind you, bro" was all Sam said.

"He's pointing at you, like he's saying, 'that's what I'm doing now.' Give me a second here . . . Charlie's pulling something out of the box again. Whoa. This is weird, but it looks like a tennis or basketball shoe. Just one. Does that make any sense to you, Sam?"

Sam laughed. "Ah, yeah. We went to a George Carlin show years ago, and Carlin talked about seeing one shoe on the side of the road, and asking, 'Why is there always just one shoe? Is someone driving along, and thinking, guess I don't need *this* one!' "

Kelly laughed. "That's funny!"

"Charlie thought it was funny too. It became a thing with us."

"Now he's running with it, like he's saying, 'I'm still running with you, bro.' "

All Sam could do was shake his head. "You *are* the real deal, Kelly!" So were the tears rolling down his cheeks.

"Alright. Now he's taking out a little green . . . leprechaun-looking doll, and holding it. Oh my. He's showing me . . . feels like a life the two of you had together. Looks like . . . Ireland. Scotland, maybe. Yeah. He says he was your older brother, and he often took care of you. It was a hard life. Looks like it's maybe just the two of you, and your mother."

Maggie squeezed his hand and winked. "Always thought ya were one of us, Sam."

"He's showing . . . you looking up to him, like you admired him so much. Loved him greatly."

"Oh my God! That's why we connected instantly in second grade. Why I could rely on him so much. Amazing!" he said as he sat back in his chair, taking in this whole new epiphany. He turned to Maggie. "Maybe that's why I feel so much at home at Finnegan's!"

"He says he saw you at the accident. Your screaming. He was trying to let you know he was okay. He's laughing; I'm seeing him leaning back, with his arms crossing his chest, and a big smile on his face, like he's saying, 'I'm really proud of you, little brother! What you did in college.' He's showing me . . . like a basketball court, and giving a thumbs up. 'Good hoo . . . hoops,' I think he's saying. He's proud of how far you've come. What you're doing with your life . . . 'Keep spreading the word,' he says.

"Ha!" Kelly laughed. "This is so sweet! He wants you to know that he really likes, and he's pointing to you, Maggie . . . now he's holding on to himself like, 'Don't be an idiot and let her go, bro!' And gives another thumbs up."

At that, Sam looked at Maggie's smile. A look that said, *I know, bro. I know.*

Kelly suddenly looked astonished, like she wasn't sure what to do with what she was now taking in. "Well, looks like that's not the *only* reason."

"What do ya mean?" asked Maggie.

At this point, Kelly closed her eyes again, and turned her head slightly. "One, two . . . three. I'm seeing three lives that you two have had together. Oh . . . maybe more."

"What are you talking about?" Sam and Maggie asked at the same time.

"Let me back up. I know this is a lot to take in. Over the many years I've been doing this, I've been reminded that the soul is eternal. I mentioned in the show about how souls from the other side tell us that they now see life here as a school for the soul. We come here to learn, grow from our experiences. Well, we can't do all the growing and learning we need to do in just one brief life. Growth, maturing is an eternal process. I've learned through the souls I've channeled that we come here many, many times. Each life has its own purpose in our growth. Does that make sense?"

Maggie nodded. "Yeah . . . it does!"

". . . Give me a minute here . . . you've been different things to each other. Brother and sister . . . one that looks like a parent/child relationship. Oh . . . you've been husband and wife to each other . . . Ooh. More than once.

"The life I'm seeing now where you were married . . . looks like a shorter time. Maggie . . . your name was . . . I'm hearing . . . seeing an E. Erin, in that life.

"Sam, you died fairly young. I see two children . . . a boy and a girl."

"Whoa," Maggie said, as she sat back in her chair. "Whoa. Magic!"

The three sat in silence. Sam and Maggie trying to absorb everything, while Kelly was taking in what was meant for her to relay.

"Okay." Kelly nodded. "I'm back with Charlie now. He's taking a jersey out of the box. He's pointing to a number . . . twelve."

"His number in high school." Sam nodded.

Kelly looked at Sam, giving him the time he needed. "You okay, Sam?"

He took a deep Coach Ferguson kind of breath. "Yeah. It's a lot."

Kelly looked over at Maggie, and smiled. "Caleb's just waiting. He seems like a patient soul."

"That he was. Is. I guess."

Kelly looks to her right, like she's listening to Caleb. "He's very happy you are here. He wants you to know that it's so beautiful there . . . 'only love . . .' He keeps repeating . . . 'only love.' " At that, Sam held Maggie's hand.

"He's telling me that he knows the pain you went through after he passed. He was with you. Always trying to comfort you. . . . Now he's showing me a little boy, and then a woman . . . he's carrying them out of a house where there's a lot of smoke."

"Oh my goodness." Maggie cried. "He got those two out of their house. There were others, in other fires."

Kelly closed her eyes. Now I see a clock he's holding . . . 'We had our time, and it was beautiful. But . . .' now he's showing me a flower . . . looks like a sunflower."

"Hmm," Maggie said. "I don't know what that's about."

"That's fine," Kelly reassured her. "That happens. Maybe it will make some kind of sense to you later.

"Give me a minute here. Now he's . . . oh my! He's holding three little souls in his arms. They're so tiny! Does that mean anything to you, Maggie?"

"Oh my God!" Maggie shouted out, as she held her face in her hands and wept. Sam put his arm around her, as he and Kelly gave her time.

"I . . . we, had three miscarriages."

Kelly leaned forward. "Oh. I'm so sorry, Maggie!" She sat back in her chair. "He's definitely letting me know that they are just fine.

They're often with him. Now he's showing me . . . it looks like a larger community . . . they're all loving them as well."

"Oh my God," Maggie kept saying. "Thank ya. Thank ya so much!"

"Oh . . . I don't know what this is about. Now he's showing me a . . . looks like a . . . yeah, it's a card. Like a playing card. He's holding it up . . . an ace of hearts. Does that mean anything to you, Maggie?"

"Oh, Caleb!" Maggie shouted. Sam took hold of her arm, and gently stroked it. "We had an ace of hearts on our nightstand, to remind us of the magic we knew. He used to love my card tricks."

"He's walking . . . holding the card, saying, 'Live your life. Your new life. Follow the magic. It's never left you, nor have I.'"

When the session ended, Kelly asked if they would like some time alone. Not really being able to speak, they just nodded, and Kelly left the room. After some quiet, Sam looked over at Maggie. "How are you doing?"

"I have no idea how to answer that."

"We'll just have to give ourselves some time with all this, I guess." Sam offered.

"With the magic" was all Maggie could say.

"Any of that feel weird to you? You know, off?"

Maggie shook her head. "No. Something resonated in here," she said, pointing to her gut.

"Me too."

They walked outside, and Maggie asked, "Can you come over to my house for a while? I gotta talk. Process this."

It was the first he had seen of Maggie's home. When he walked through the door, he was struck by how minimalistic it all looked. "We both liked to keep it simple in regard to material things. Found it helped us focus on the important stuff," Maggie explained as they walked toward the kitchen.

Pictures and artwork were prominent. Pictures of Maggie's family, and the home and area she grew up in. Beautiful paintings, Sam assumed were Caleb's. Other artwork, Maggie would later explain, were gifts from Caleb's artist friends. It was clear that only the meaningful, only what was from the heart, took up space in Maggie O'Brien's home.

"I think maybe I understand it now. This draw I feel to you," Sam said as Maggie walked into the porch off the kitchen with some tea. "At least some of it."

Maggie looked across the room at the picture of her home in Howth. "Stories. They come and go," she muttered. "Strange territory. Knowing what we think we know now. It's a new kind of magic. This feeling we know." Turning to Sam, she said, "I don't know what to do with this."

"I don't either. A week ago, I wasn't into this whole medium thing at all. Hearing from the dead. It's a lot, but I do know I like it. It's fascinating. Who'd a thunk?"

"So . . . where do we go from here?"

"I guess . . . we just have to be *here* . . . now . . . I'll be Sam. You be Maggie. Everything *this* life is. Whatever this time brings."

"Yeah, I guess. It feels different though now. Doesn't it, Sam?"

"That it does," Sam said, hearing Maggie's whisper in the words.

Silence.

"Sam. Ya remember when ya got out of my car that first night we were together, and I said your name, and then said, 'never mind'?"

"Yeah."

She felt the tears welling up. "What I wanted to say was 'Why does it feel like I've just come home?' I guess I know now."

"Yeah. I'm feeling that too."

"Sam, if what Kelly told us is true, and it feels like it is . . . about us being husband and wife in other lifetimes . . . then this isn't the first time we've sat together in a house."

"Yeah, I suppose."

With that, they sat in silence. Being and doing what they apparently had done countless times before. Perhaps remembering a little of what they once were. Discovering what they are now.

Sam's eyes settled on a picture on the piano. "Caleb?"

"Yeah."

"I can see he's everything you described."

"That he was. Is, I guess I should say now. There were so many days, especially the first months, that I just sat here, staring at it. Sometimes speakin' to it. Helped me feel like I was really talkin' to him."

After looking at it for a moment, she said, "Oh my goodness! I really was!"

"I used to do the same with Charlie. Felt weird doing it, so I only did it when I was sure no one was around. But it helped."

"When I'd look at his picture, I felt everything I did when I looked at him when he was here. Those eyes always drew me in. I'd often look into them and ask, "What's going on in there, Caleb?"

"Did he always let you in?"

"Oh yeah. Most of the time. Don't we all have things we keep to ourselves? For sure *I* do. I think it's good we have our own things sometimes."

Instantly a recurring thought popped up for Sam. *Haven't told Maggie about the reason for the divorce. Now? Don't want to. Way too much for one day. Gotta do it. She deserves to know.*

The embrace at the door, when Sam was leaving, felt like a first. No words to describe it. Something was different. They both knew it. Can people know a first kiss twice? *They* did. One filled now with a shared history. A forgotten knowing of what had been, and a growing sense of what is now. It was a step toward home.

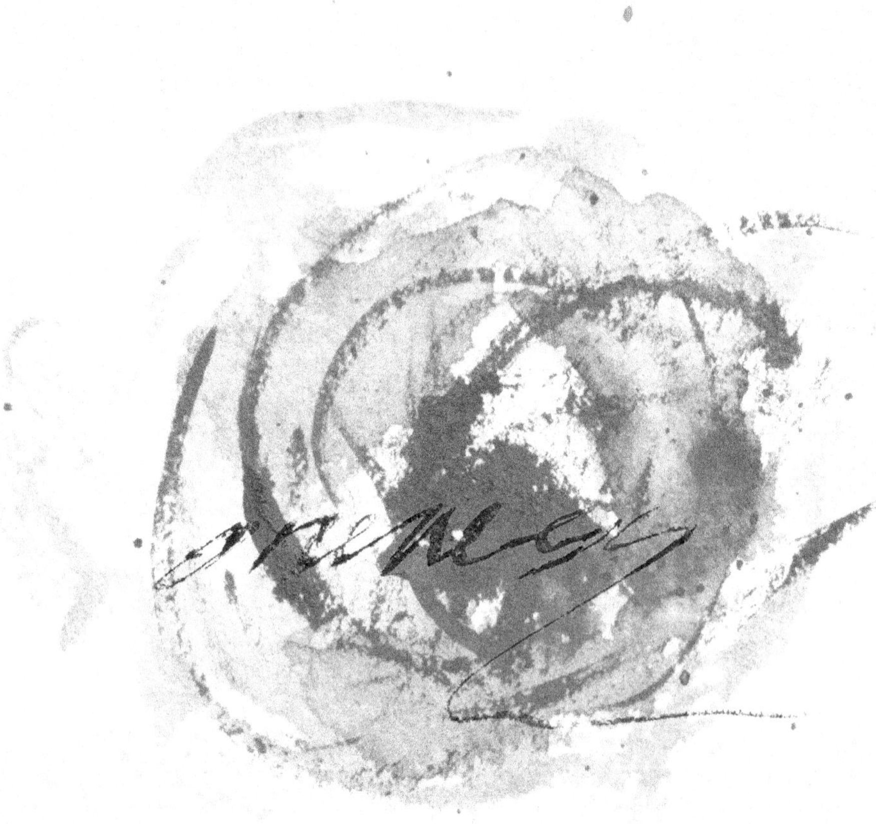

17

In a Time Such as This

"SHE WHAT?"

It was an early Sunday morning call from Sol while Sam was on his way to the station. The woman who was to be Sam's guest that morning, Elizabeth Sheldon, a political commentator, had suddenly died while at her daughter Paige's home the night before. Remembering that her mom was to be on the show, Paige contacted the station's 24/7 messaging service.

"Oh my God! I just talked with her yesterday!"

Sol had already put up his white flag. "We'll just go to a rerun, Sam. It's all we can do this late in the game."

"No!" Sam suddenly heard himself say.

"What do you mean, no? You're on the air in four hours!"

"I know! Sol, I told everyone last week that Elizabeth was going to be our guest today. She's got a loyal following. If we go to a rerun they'll wonder why she's not here. No, I've got this. I'll fill the guest slot myself. We'll stick with what Elizabeth and I were planning on talking about. The whole 'living in these political times' thing. I pretty much know what I'll do with it. Yeah . . . this will work!"

"But what . . . okay, Sam. Just say she was unable to be with us this morning. We can't say what happened. There's probably still family to notify."

Unable to be with us. Sam thought of the reading he and Maggie had with Kelly, the medium. *Maybe she will be.*

"Five minutes, everyone!" Carly announced. Five minutes. For Sam, it felt like that was all the time he had to come up with something. But when you know, you know. Well, you hope so.

Carly: Right here. *Five, four, three . . .*

Sam: Good morning everyone. And welcome to this Sunday's edition of *You Are Love*. I'm your host, Sam Crawford.

It was then that Sam went blank. There was no type on the teleprompter. There hadn't been time to rewrite it. He was on his own. It was probably only ten seconds, but ten seconds of air time is an eternity. Everyone in the crew started to look around. An already-nervous Sol leaned forward in the sound booth. "C'mon, Sam. You got this." Sam looked down at Shadow, who was telling him the same.

Our scheduled guest this morning, political commentator Elizabeth Sheldon, is unable to be with us. We had planned on discussing the current political climate. How we might go about living in the fear, chaos, anger, division, and uncertainty we're all experiencing now. That will still be our focus this morning.

No matter what our politics or beliefs may be, I think at least most of us would agree that we are at another major crossroads in our country. What we do with this time will not only determine the direction of the country, but also the kind of lives those dearest to us will experience for quite some time.

He paused, wondering if he should say what he wanted to say. He quickly decided he had no choice.

Our country's gone through threats to our democracy and our freedoms before, but none quite like the threats we're experiencing in these times.

And then the silent airspace began again… "C'mon Sam. What do you have?" Sol muttered. Sam looked down at Shadow again. He saw a flash of the moment they first met, and found the words.

If we are to know the truth of anything, I believe we must go back to its beginning. It is there that its truth is pure, unaltered by human agendas and limitations. I'd like to bring us back to our first show. My guest provided for us an image that you now see on your screen. You may remember this.

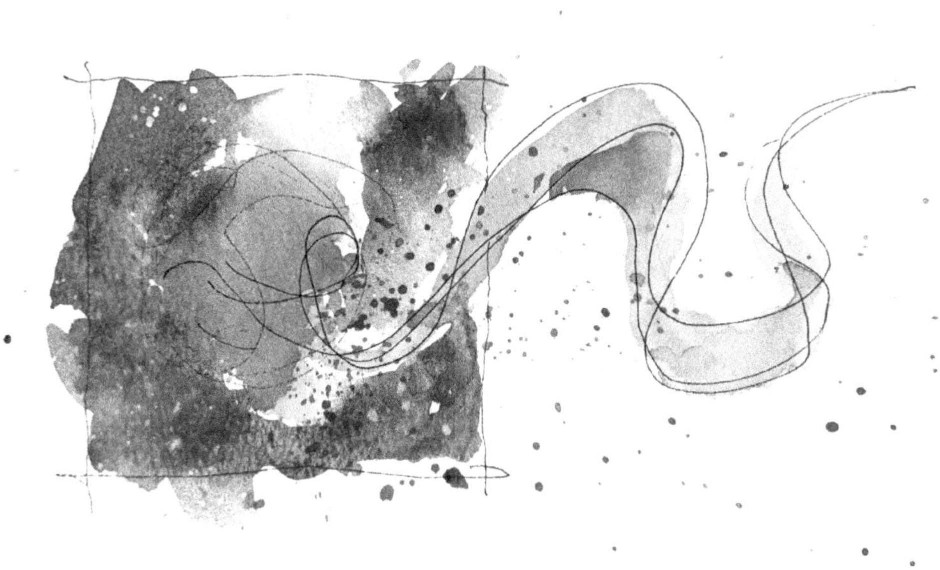

It's an image of the beginning, fundamental truth of all reality. It's an image depicting energy. Science has long been telling us that everything is essentially energy. That energy must have a Source. The energy Source you're looking at right now is an attempt to visualize everything that is, coming out of the interior of this One Source.

Now, this is a spiritually based show. And we're intentional on *You Are Love* to not *name* this spiritual energy and associate it with any religion, or one particular religion.

We want you *all* to feel included in what's presented here. Because you *are* included in what this image shows. *All* of us are.

Now, everything that comes out of this One Source *is* the Source. Made of the same essence as this Source, which we affirm is love. Thus, the name of this show—*You Are Love.*

And here is where this can begin to shape how we live and see one another in these fractured and scary times. Look closely again. There is an inherent, natural Oneness in all that is.

You see the little gold spots coming out of the Source. Those represent everything that is. This morning, think of them as souls. No one *has* a soul. Everyone *is* a soul. A unique, but universal, spiritual energy.

At this point, Sam stopped.

Can we take a moment, and let that soak in . . .

I don't know what your politics are. That's *your* concern. But does it make sense to look to this Source of everything for the *source* of our politics? This infinite Source of intelligence that created the universe and makes it all work. This infinite Source of wisdom we *all* come from. This Source that *precedes* politics. *Precedes* country, race, religion, and economic status. It makes sense to me. How about you?

Sol spoke into Sam's earpiece. "Sam, I like where you're going with this. Just stay with it." Normally, Sam would be upset with the interruption, but not today. He welcomed the encouragement.

Are you curious about what the intelligence of this infinite spiritual energy knows? What does it know that *we* aren't aware of? What does it know about the best way forward for us, living in the darkness of our limitations? What can it *see* that we can't see?

Sam turned to camera right.

I find myself wanting its eyes.

To be able to look through *its eyes,* and see the immigrant the way *it* sees and knows the immigrant.

To be able to see the human concepts of country and borders as *it* sees and knows them.

To be able to see and understand race, religion, and economic status the way *it* sees and understands them.

To be able to see those different from me, those who anger and frustrate me, through *its* sacred eyes.

I ask myself, what would be my perspective from *that* vantage point?

For me, all of it begs the question, how would I ever be able to see with those eyes?

It seems something in me must be able to, at least somewhat! Otherwise, why do I want it? Where does the wanting come from?

I'm slowly starting to see that those eyes *are* in our soul. Our heart. Spiritual teachers call it the third eye. It's there, if we're willing to go deep and see . . . for ourselves.

The Heart of the Conversation

I have a daughter, Avery, who has Down syndrome. Who, in her own way, has those eyes.

She naturally accepts. Connects. I sometimes ask myself when I'm with her, who is the "challenged" one here? I've come to realize it's *me.*

I just felt my heart when I spoke of Avery . . .

By this time, tears were welling up in Sam's eyes, and it was the viewers turn to feel the heart he was speaking from. He paused again, and pointed to his head.

I'm spending way too much time in here, spinning the same thoughts, endless opinions, and judgments that I'm so convinced to be true. Not really getting anywhere. Leaving me only exhausted. *[He shook his head.]* No. The mind alone can't lead. It's far too limited and clouded by its fear.

Sam put his hand back on his heart.

We need a much wiser one to lead us. It's the light in our hearts that can *first* show us the best way forward, and show us what is wisest to say and do. I need to trust my heart.

Be quiet, let go, be present to it, and listen.

We may be confused or in despair over what to do. When I do *something*, the light within is showing and nudging me. It's there that I notice hope rising up again into my consciousness. A hope I realize has never left me. Makes sense I guess, considering what we all come from, that it couldn't really leave. Hope is what we all *are*. So act however *you* are led, my friends.

For me, I seek to go forward in the light of the truths dearest to *my* heart—

We are all naturally One with our Source,
each other, and everything around us,

and

We are all love.

> I welcome your comments and thoughts regarding what I've shared today. You can contact me through the email below. Thank you for listening. What I've shared with you this morning is mine. The show today came together very quickly. No one in management or ownership had time to know what I would say. I thank them for their trust.

Sam could barely utter the next words.

> It's vital we find our community and hold them close.
>
> "We're all just walking each other home."
>
> May you always remember. You are love. Love is the only way forward.

Sam sits back in his chair and sobs. In the midst of it, Sol tries to console him. "Okay, Sam. Thank you. We'll see how they respond."

One minute after the show ended, Maggie texted.

> Oh dear Sam! Absolutely lovely! So proud of you. Charlie is too!

By Sunday evening, the following appeared on Sam's work email.

> Thank you, Sam. I needed that. Gives me hope. Love the show!
>
> Bravo, Sam! Thank you for being so vulnerable. It's up to us!
>
> Another bleeding heart, liberal crock of bullshit. Crawford, you're an idiot! Wake up! Wait. You're already too woke!
>
> Thanks, Sam. I struggle so much with my anger over what's happening these days.

I recently saw a piece that CBS Sunday morning did on The Litowitz Center for Enlightened Disagreement at Northwestern University. Its cofounder, Professor Eli Finkel, said they give their students the assignment of listening for what the other person values as they express their strong opinions or what's upsetting them. That made sense to me. If we did that, I think we'd often see the one we disagree with in a more humane light, and maybe find that we value at least some of the same things.

Great message. Hard to live. But we need to try.

I'll never watch your show again. What a bunch of shit!

I'm sure we disagree politically, but I appreciate your trying to help us come together. You're right. Love is the answer. Love *is* our deepest truth, and the only way forward. We *can* do this! In the spirit of your message, I wish you well, Sam.

I'm scared for our country. Some days I'm in complete despair. Thank you for pointing the way forward. I love "act toward hopefulness." Maybe there *is* a future for us all.

I'm trying so hard not to think we're screwed. Gonna think about what you said.

Oversimplified. Naive. Wake up to the real world!

A light in the darkness. A way forward. Thank you!

Coming from the "spiritual, but not religious" crowd, I appreciate how included I feel as I listen to your show. Thank you for speaking from your heart.

I wish you'd talk more about Jesus on your show. He's the only way to salvation. But I liked some parts of your message.

Texts appeared from four women in the ownership group later that evening.

> I applaud you, Sam! Thank you for your courage and insight.
>
> Sam, you spoke eloquently and clearly from your heart. KLUV is lucky to have you.
>
> I watched your show this morning with a grateful heart. *This* is why I am invested in KLUV. We carry on!
>
> Proud of you, Sam. Proud of KLUV. I would love to have coffee with you this week. Please give me a call.

18

We Need to Talk. Part Three

MAGGIE, I WON'T SAY WE NEED TO TALK. That always sounds concerning.

It's just that I have something I really need to tell you about. Can we do it soon? Tonight? If you're available.

That was the text Sam left for Maggie right after the show. He wanted to arrange getting together that night at Finnegan's.

Sam sat anxiously in the Sheehan room where he had asked Maggie to meet him. Hoping it would work its peaceful magic. He was glad that it looked like they would be alone. He needed privacy to tell her what he felt he had kept private for far too long. It really hadn't been that long since they had met. But the waiting, the wondering when Maggie would ask about his marriage and divorce, only *seemed* to make it an eternity.

Watching Maggie walk in only reminded him of what he could lose that night. Hope. Excitement that had been missing. He gave her a long hug.

"Okay, Sam. I'm a wee bit nervous here. What is it?"

"I'm sorry." *Aw shit, this is hard,* he thought.

"Maggie, I need to talk with you about my marriage and divorce. You've been very kind and patient with me in not asking me about it. Thank you."

"I thought ya would tell me when ya were ready."

"Well, I am. There's something you deserve to know before this goes any further. If it does, after tonight.

"Maggie, I remember you told me that first night up on the bluff that we all put on a show. I'm not only the guy I've been showing you. I've made my mistakes, and one very bad one.

"I could go into the details, but I don't want to give the impression they are excuses. They're not. There *is* no excuse."

Looking across the Sheehan, perhaps trying to evoke some of its magic, he took another deep breath. "About three years ago, I . . . had an affair." Tears welled up in his eyes. Tears that were becoming all too familiar in an all-too-familiar conversation. "It was pure stupidity. I've regretted it ever since. More than I can say. I hurt my family deeply. Jadyn is a wonderful woman and mother. I adore my kids. It cost me everything that mattered to me, although I deserved it." With that, Sam sat back in his chair, looking only at the table. He couldn't get himself to look up.

Maggie kept her gaze on Sam for a while. "Excuse me," she said as she stood up and slowly walked over to a painting of an Irish family, standing in front of their farmhouse in Ireland. She stood there, keeping her eyes on the painting. "I sometimes come here and imagine what their story might be. One time, that little girl is having a grand adventure. Another time, the boy just recovered from a serious illness. His parents were so worried they'd lose him. I imagine how the husband and wife first met. The parents' stern look sometimes speaks to me of a disappointing harvest. I imagine the love within the family. How they stuck together through it all." She kept staring for another minute.

"The point is," she said as she walked back to their table and sat down, "we make choices, Sam, as to what our story will be. Our stories are a series of choices. We can't decide everything. Caleb taught me that. But even there, we can choose how we respond."

She took Sam's hand, looking far into him, as if she was looking to be sure she had reason to trust her heart. "And if this continues, I'm choosing to trust ya." Taking his other hand, she spoke from the depths of those green eyes. "I'll be honest. This is hard for me to hear.

We Irish are family people." Her voice trailed off as she stared back at the painting. "We're family people. But it's hard for another reason."

She looked around the Sheehan, and turned back to Sam. "There was a time when I was afraid of how close I was to doing the same thing. I know I've talked of how magical Caleb and I were together. And it's mostly true. But we went through a couple of rough patches. Little connection. There was a lad in the band, and during one of those times, I was growing afraid of how much I felt myself drawn to him. We never crossed that line. I knew I couldn't do that to Caleb. I loved him too much. But I know part of me wanted to." She paused and shook her head. "It scared me."

She looked back at the painting. "I never told Caleb. I knew it would break his heart. I couldn't lose him. In a strange way, now that he's gone, I feel worse about it. Gone is my chance to come clean with him. Anyway, the guy was married too, and we decided one of us had to leave the band. He volunteered to leave what he loved so much."

She leaned into Sam. "Sam, I have no real ground to stand on to judge ya. But I must tell ya this. If we continue, and ya did that to me, it's over. I can't have it any other way."

"I understand, Maggie. Of course. I know I would never do that again."

"Do we ever *really* know, Sam?"

As if he was checking what anyone can know for sure, Sam looked back into her eyes.

"I *think* I do. But I suppose the raw truth is, no. Not really."

She took hold of both his hands. This time the deeper green in her eyes revealed an even deeper vulnerability. "We can only *choose* who we'll put our trust in, Sam."

Sam got up and held her. "This is *such* a relief! I came here so afraid that you'd walk out. Never want to see me again. You'd have every right to."

"I suppose I would. But so would ya. Now that ya know this about me, can ya trust *me*?"

Sam didn't miss a beat. "Yes. I can. You're incredible, Maggie O'Brien."

"As are ya. It took great courage for ya to tell me this."

Sam took a deep breath, as if taking in what Maggie had just given him. "I feel so much lighter," Sam said. "This secret that's been with us is out there now. I can't thank you enough."

"Thank *ya,* Sam, for valuing me and what we're discovering we have enough to do the hard thing."

"You want to walk downtown for a while?"

"Sure, Sam. I could use some air."

And so they did. It would become something that was theirs to do. Maggie shopped only the family-owned businesses. She loved regaling Sam with family stories told to her. Calling the storefronts "storyfronts" as they strolled along.

They ended up back at the overlook on the bluff that night. Something that would become their thing as well. Being high above the city and creating stories together. Maggie's spot becoming *theirs.*

Maggie: See the gray house, next to that grove of trees? That guy likes to walk around in his house singing country-western.

Sam: In his underwear!

Look at that Prius going by the park! She doesn't know it yet, but the valet gave her the wrong one.

Maggie: The dead body should be a clue.

That hideous blue house with the white fence around it. The neighbors snuck over and painted it one night.

Sam: It's a small world. But I wouldn't want to paint it . . . *Steven Wright.*

I think that woman in the brown house works from home.

Maggie: Probably CIA.

Sam: Or PTA.

Maggie: The PTA is a cover for the CIA.

Sam: When we were married in another life, you suppose we lived in a house like that one by the park with the front porch?

Maggie: Nah. Ours had a wraparound porch. Always wanted one of those.

H 9.5 V
82 82

19

A Little Closer to Ben

THE END OF FEBRUARY 2026 ARRIVED, and Ben's season was coming to a close. Charlie RAV4 was bringing Sam to his last home game. They set up getting together at a restaurant on the edge of campus after the game. Ben texted that he had something he wanted to talk about.

As soon as he entered the arena, it all came flooding back. The crowd filling up the place. The cheerleaders. The band playing music that fired up the crowd, and the warm-up. Ben got him a good seat near courtside. As he sat down, he even caught himself looking for Booker, his old teammate.

It came time for Ben to be introduced among the starting five before tipoff. Sam stood proudly and couldn't help but say to the woman next to him, "That's my boy!"

"You must be so proud," she said.

"That I am!" he responded, hearing Maggie in the cadence.

The game was pure connection for Sam. His ups and downs in sync with every one of his son's.

"C'mon, Ben! You got this," Sam yelled when Ben was at the line for a free throw. The words came out at a fairly quiet moment, as Ben started to focus on the rim. *Crap, Crawford. Shut up!* He knew how he always hated the distraction when he was at the line.

With thirty seconds left, the score was tied. Ben was having a good game. Fifteen points and twelve rebounds. Three blocks. After a timeout, Ben's team ran a play that would get the ball inside to him, to drive to the basket. It worked perfectly. Ben took a great pass from his point guard and took two steps toward the rim. He had a half step on his defender and went up for the shot. The crowd groaned as the ball bounced off the rim to an opposing player, who lobbed the ball down court to a teammate for an even easier layup. Game over.

Given the outcome of the game, Ben opted to meet with his dad at The Improper Fraction, a half mile *off* campus. Sam didn't have to wonder about what he'd say, as he waited for Ben. He knew what he would have wanted from *his* dad. Nothing. Except, "I'm sorry, son. Tough break." But it's hard to tell your son things like that when you're never there.

Ben eventually walked in. Sam stood to greet him, hoping to give his son a hug, but Ben just plopped into the booth.

"I'm sorry, son. Tough break."

Ben shook his head. "God! It was right there!"

It took a while for the conversation to get off the game. Off of basketball. After some talk about classes and school life, Ben stopped and just stared at his dad. Looking like a blank page with so much written on it.

"You okay, Ben?"

Ben shook his head. "It's just that . . . I've been accused of plagiarism by my English lit prof." He looked into his dad's eyes, hoping for . . . well, he didn't know.

"I didn't do it!" Ben said, showing the same determined look Sam saw when his son drove to the basket that night. "I checked out the source my prof said I ripped off, and I could see the similarities. But I was just writing from me. I swear. It just came out weirdly the same. No AI. No nothin'!"

"I'm sorry, Ben. What can you do?"

"I don't know. I'm worried I could lose my scholarship. He's coming down that hard on me."

"Have you tried—"

Ben's response was quick, as if he knew what was coming. "I don't need you to fix it! I just need you to be my dad. Just hang with me!"

And it was there that father Crawford found himself in the most difficult space a parent can know. Wanting to fix, take away, protect, with none of those options available. Only waiting, hoping, and trusting his son to find his way. A father and son sharing what two men especially fear—vulnerability.

Sam gave him some time and then put his hand on his arm. "I know you'll find your way through this, and thank you for still meeting with me after a rough night. I've had a few myself. It just sucks. Is that what you wanted to talk about, Ben, or is there something else?"

Shaking his head, he said, "Yeah. Okay . . . I just can't do it. Can't get past the anger at what you did to Mom. The disappointment. I just can't let it go. I want to, but . . . damn, it's so hard. Feels crazy! It does help though seeing Mom so happy now."

"Your mom told me that you know about Laura, Ben."

"Yeah. I do. I'm happy that she's happy. But . . . never saw that coming."

"Can't say I did either. But I'm happy for her too."

Ben looked straight into his father's eyes and leaned forward. "Shit! I had this image of you, and you just blew it to hell. I think . . . because I looked up to you so much, it's even harder. I wanted more from you. I've hated you for all the hurt you've caused!

"I understand."

"No! That's just it, Dad. I don't think you do. How could you?"

Sam once again took in the bitter disappointment in his son's eyes. "Ben, I'm so sorry for the immense pain I've caused you, Avery, and your mom. It breaks my heart to know what you've been feeling toward me. I deserve all of your anger."

It was then he looked away for a moment, checking in to see if this was the right time. Knowing it was, he opened up to Ben about how he had felt being around his dad growing up. He told Ben what a mean drunk he was. He replayed what happened that day in the upstairs hallway when he was five, getting slammed into the wall by his dad. His own constant and bitter disappointment in who his father was. His dad never showing up to his games, and how painfully disappointed he always was in his dad.

He didn't say it, but Ben knew he had just seen a place where he could truly meet his dad. The words "painfully disappointed" brought him there. "I had no idea" was all he said.

"Of course you didn't. I never told you," Sam said, closing his eyes. "I hated him, Ben, just like you hate me. In my better days, when I wasn't consumed by my anger, I'd think there had to be something awful in his story for him to be like he was. I visited him recently in Fillmore, where he lives. We talked, and he let me into his story for the first time."

After sharing what his dad had told him, Sam could feel they both needed a moment. "Finding myself in his story for the first time, I felt safe in his vulnerability, I guess. Safe enough to talk about how I really felt being around him growing up. Turns out he knew, all along, but not like he does now."

Sam shook his head as he told his son, "I've been wanting to know the truth of his story my whole life. Now that he finally told me . . . I don't know . . . this all feels so new and strange for me. For the first time in my life, my father showed me the way by being real and vulnerable. He's shown me the way in opening up to you." Sam leaned toward his son. "I hate that I've given you reason to feel what I always felt."

They sat for a few moments, feeling the harsh reality they shared, with Sam feeling strangely closer to Ben.

"Ben, I miss you so much! And as hard as it may be to believe, I loved you before you were even born."

Feeling overwhelmed with his emotions, Ben got up to leave. Sam quickly asked, "Can I come and see you again this spring? Maybe shoot some hoops?"

As tears welled up in his eyes, Ben could only whisper, "Yeah. Sure."

"I don't know how to do this either, Ben. I hope we can find our way. You had what? Twelve rebounds? Blocked three shots. Fifteen points. We only focus on the shots that are missed. I know that all too well. I'm so proud of you, Ben. Right behind you."

As Ben walked away, Sam asked. "Did you hear me yell when you were at the line?"

"Yeah. Hate that . . . don't do that!"

"I know. I always hated it, too. Sorry! Won't happen again!"

20

Walking Each Other Home

SOME NIGHTS WALK YOU HOME like no other. This night in March began with meeting wisdom in a sweet, gentle old man.

Sam sat at Finnegan's well before the Irish Way would take the stage that Friday night, waiting for his Irish stew. And there he was! Angus McGee. Sitting by himself, with a gentle smile that looked like it knew things no one else knew. The very person Maggie urged him to meet.

"Angus?" the tall guy said, walking toward him.

"Yes, lad!"

"Good evening. I'm . . ."

"Sam Crawford, wouldn't ya be?"

"Yes, sir."

"I've watched ya show on the TV. Here, have a seat, lad."

"You sure?"

"Well, there's a few things I'm sure of, and this is one of 'em!" He stood and put out his hand. "It's a pleasure to meet ya, Sam. Angus. Angus McGee."

"Yes. Maggie, who sings in the Irish Way, told me I've got to do myself a favor and meet you."

"Oh the favor is mine, dear Sam. You know Maggie?"

"Ah. Yeah. Getting there."

"Oh. She's a wonderful girl. Ya'd do well to get to know her!" said the twinkle in Angus's eye.

"Well said. So. You live around here often?"

"Say what?"

"Sorry, Angus. Old joke. I hear you're a regular at Finnegan's."

"Oh yeah. Especially after my dear Katie passed. It's good company."

"How long have you been in Newcastle?"

"Moved here from Ireland as a young lad. Never left. Born in Ireland in 1928."

"So you're . . ."

"Ninety-eight years young, my friend."

"You don't look it!"

"Keep smilin', lad," he said. "And be kind. It'll get ya ninety-eight trips around the sun, I like to say!"

"Is that the second thing you know, Angus?"

"Yup. That, and if fortune shines on ya, and a good woman comes into your life, don't let her go."

Sam tilted his head a bit. *Hmm. Second person to tell me that.*

"Sounds like *you* did, Angus."

"That I did. Katie was me light. Love of me life. She got me through a whole lot of cac."

"Ah yes." Sam nodded, lifting his pint. "Good old cac. There's a lot of it going around these days."

"Oh, it's everywhere, Sam! But I tell ya, you find your Katie, and y'all be just fine."

"Tell me about her."

"I met her here, actually. We were both in our early twenties. June 12, 1948, it was. Saw her across the way, and awww, I just knew," Angus said, leaning toward Sam. "Took me the whole night to get up me courage, but me lads pushed me over to her.

"Best thing I ever did," he said as he sat back in his chair. "She showed me the way, and the wisdom of a smile. God . . . her smile! Showed me what a kind word can do. The magic of compassion in the eye."

"Magic, huh?"

"That it was. Pure magic. And oh me God, she could laugh and tell a spicy joke better than any lad. God, how she made people laugh!

I think that's how we made it so long. Laughed our way through!" Angus said as he lifted his pint.

"How long were you together?"

"Made it to seventy years, before the cancer took her."

"When did she pass?"

"Almost six years ago now. Part of me left with her, Sam. It's not the same. *I'm* not the same. I miss her every day."

Angus looked across the room. "I can still look over there and see her," he said, pointing to the far end of the Daley. "She's still as beautiful as ever." At that, Sam watched that magical night play itself out all over again in Angus's mind. He watched Angus walk over and introduce himself. "She had a beautiful blue dress on. A white-and-gold necklace that made her look like a princess. And, ay, that smile. Melt any lad's heart. Did mine for sure. She never stopped. Guess that's why I come here so often. To say hello to Katie, all over again."

Sam felt like he wanted to let Angus stay there for a while, and not interrupt this precious reunion. When it felt right, Sam smiled. "You're a lucky man, Angus McGee."

"Indeed I am. Ye got your own Katie?"

"Well, I did. Thinking these days that I may have found her again."

"Sounds like there's a lot in that story!"

"There is, to be sure."

"You live here in Newcastle, Sam?"

"Yeah. On Kensington Drive. On the Willoughby."

"Kensington? My folks eventually built a home there. What's the address?"

"1242."

"Holy cac, Sam! That's the house they built! I grew up there! Jaysus, Mary, and Joseph!"

"Are you kidding me, Angus? It's a big house. Big family?"

"Eight siblings. They're all gone now. Last one passed a few months ago."

"You've had a lot of loss, Angus. I'm sorry."

"That I have. Part of the deal when ya make it to ninety-eight." He smiled. "Every loss tells me how much I gained."

"What was it like growing up in that house?"

"Wild. Me brothers and I played mostly outside. Mother wouldn't let us destroy the house! Although we did lower each other out from more than one window, I'll tell ya that! My sisters loved to be in the den on the first floor. Or upstairs. Playing house, and so on. My dad made his money in lumber, and then mining. He wasn't around all that much. Kind of a harsh sort of man. Never felt really close. Mother ... she was a good one."

"Yeah, kind of know what you mean, Angus."

"That's a big house. You alone in there, Sam?"

"I'm on the first floor. KLUV refurbished the place. Gives me a home for the time being."

"Ah yes. I heard it's really nice in there now, again. Glad to hear of it."

"Angus, you mind if I stay at your table and eat dinner with you?"

"Love it, my new friend! Appreciate the good company."

During dinner, Angus's heart kept speaking of Katie's "magic." Sam thought about that word that keeps popping into his life now, and the one who is bringing it to him. People kept stopping by Angus's table. It was like they couldn't get enough of him. Magic will do that.

Sam and Angus took a small table near the front of the stage as the show was about to start. The Irish Way came on, greeted by their raucous fans.

"Good love to ye!" Maggie shouted. "We're grateful for ye, and to be here again at this second home for us all, Finnegan's!"

"Yeah!" The crowd shouted and clapped. Song suggestions were yelled toward the stage.

"Oh my! You got that playlist, lads?" Maggie said, turning to the band. "We'll get to some of 'em. But first, how about we sail from 'Paddy's Green Shamrock Shore.'"

"Take us away, Maggie!"

From Derry quay we sailed away on the twenty-third of May
We were taken on board by a pleasant crew, bound for Amerikay.
Fresh water then we did take on, five thousand gallons or more.
In case we'd run short going to New York far away from the shamrock shore ...
So fare thee well, sweet Liza dear and likewise to Derry Town,
and twice farewell to my comrades brave who dwell on that sainted ground.
If fortune it ever should favor me, and I to have money in store.
I'll come back and I'll wed the wee lassie I left on Paddy's Green Shamrock Shore.

When the song ended, Maggie reached over and grabbed a pint on stage. "To Paddy!"

"To Paddy!" the crowd cheered.

Angus watched Sam during the song, and leaned over. "She your Katie?"

Sam looked a little flustered. "That obvious?"

Angus lifted his Guinness and winked. "I wish ya well, lad."

"Well, I'd like to introduce my wonderful comrades up here with me tonight," she shouted. "You all know Danny. On fiddle for that song.

"Sean, on flute.

"Eric on guitar.

"And back with us tonight, on bodhrán and fiddle, an old friend and former band member, Liam McDervish. Welcome back, Liam!"

After a few more songs, Angus knew something was bothering Sam. At the break he asked, "Ya okay, Sam? Ye seemed sidetracked there for a bit."

"Nah. Just thinking."

Angus didn't buy it. Ninety-eight trips will do that to you.

Liam began the second set by being lead singer for "Whiskey in the Jar."

As I was going over the far-famed Kerry mountains
I met with Captain Farrel and his money he was counting.
I first produced my pistol, and then produced my rapier.
Said stand and deliver, for I am a bold deceiver.

The crowd joined in the chorus:

musha ring dumma do damma da
whack for the daddy 'ol
whack for the daddy 'ol
there's whiskey in the jar

Now some men take delight in the drinking and the roving,
But others take delight in the gambling and the smoking.
But I take delight in the juice of the barley,
And courting pretty maids in the morning bright and early

musha ring dumma do damma da
whack for the daddy 'ol
whack for the daddy 'ol
there's whiskey in the jar

Sam Crawford knew about competition. Winning and losing. And it all rose up in him that night. Just as it did when he went center court for the jump ball starting a game. Liam was handsome, with dark red hair that was beginning to gray a bit. Square chin. Big shoulders. The whole nine yards. Maybe even ten. All Sam thought was *He's got game.*

The show ended as it always did for the Irish Way. Everyone stood and sang "The Parting Glass," with hearts full of the night.

Sam stood and shook hands with his new friend, Angus McGee. "It was an honor to meet you, sir."

Angus winked again. "Good luck, Sam Crawford."

He and Maggie had arranged to walk back to Sam's. They went past many of Maggie's favorite shops and stories downtown. Stories of chances taken. Some lost. Some gained. Maggie seemed to know them all.

She suddenly stopped and turned. "Oh, Sam!" she said with a shout that startled him.

"What?"

"Sorry, but I forgot to tell ya. Remember when we were at the reading with Kelly, and she said that she was seein' a picture of a sunflower?"

"Yeah, and you didn't know what that was about."

"A couple of days later I was in the basement, where Caleb did his painting. I was going through them, and I saw this gorgeous painting he did of a sunflower. He named it 'Maggie.' I just stood there with it in my hands, bawlin' my eyes out. Called me his 'sunshine' for a while after he finished it! I had forgotten. How could I have forgotten something as sweet as that?"

"Whoa. That's amazing and beautiful!" Sam said. "Just take it for the gift that Caleb gave you. Twice!"

"Yeah." After some more steps into the night, Maggie shook her head. "Still overwhelmed by that whole experience, Sam!"

"Me too."

They walked a little further along Main Street until they came upon Schumann's Coffee and Bakery. "This used to be an Indian restaurant. I got to know the couple who owned it, not long after we moved here. Lovely people, and they worked so hard to make a go of it. I guess the community just wasn't ready for it."

"Everything in its own time and way, I guess," Sam said, speaking mostly to himself.

"Speaking of which, how did it go with Ben?" Maggie asked as they walked by Sullivan's clothing store.

"It was . . . felt like we both did what we both needed to do to maybe move forward. Got to tell him things about his grandfather he never knew. Hell, *I* never knew until recently. I told Ben what it was like growing up with my dad. How I felt around him. I think we shared a space we'd never shared before. 'Fuckin' vulnerability,' as my dad calls it. To tell you the truth, I felt closer to Ben than I have for a long time."

Maggie nodded, knowing all about his life with Frank Crawford from a recent three-pint conversation.

They walked awhile longer with Maggie picking up on Sam wanting to talk about Liam, but not knowing how.

"It was awkward having Liam there tonight," she said. "He's a great musician, and the lads love him. I mean awkward between us."

"Yeah. I suppose. He's really good! Knows how to work a crowd for sure!"

"That he does." She stopped, took both of Sam's hands. "There's nothin' there, Sam. That was so clear tonight. I've moved on. Not sure he has though. But I *know* I have. We needed someone to fill in for Greg quickly, and he obliged. That's all it was."

Sam smiled. "I choose to trust you." They kissed, and after Maggie shared another "storyfront," he stopped. "So do you go from store to store, saying, 'Hi! I'm Maggie O'Brien, tell me your story'?"

Maggie smiled and kissed the tall guy, thinking that only ballerinas should fall for such a guy. It's a workout for a 5'5" person's toes.

"I'm a sucker for family stories, Sam."

The plan was for Sam to give Maggie a ride back to her place. But when they got to Sam's, Maggie said, "There's something I need to tell ya about. Can I tell ya inside?" In an instant he heard Jadyn at the coffee shop. *I guess we all have our secrets, Sam.*

Once inside the den, Sam made a fire, joining Maggie on the couch.

"I fell for this lad, back in my teens. Hard," she said, looking into the fire. "It may have been a 'gray more' as my grandmother used to say. A big love. I don't know. I was awfully young.

"Anyway, I got pregnant at eighteen. The summer after I graduated. It was hard for my parents, being the proud Irish family they are.

"I knew right away what I had to do, and that I couldn't tell my parents." Staring into the fire, she nodded. "One day I got on a bus, went to a clinic, and had an abortion."

Sam nestled closer, putting his arm around her.

"It was so hard. Torn as I was between knowing how much I wanted to be a mum someday. But it was *some*day. Someday down the road. I just knew . . . I wasn't ready."

She continued telling her story to the fire. "I thought a lot about having the baby and giving it up for adoption. But I couldn't bear the thought of giving my little baby to someone else. Knowing she or he was out there. Somewhere. I pictured myself seeing a little girl or boy, and wondering, 'Is that her? Is that him?' "

As she began to cry, she forced out the words. "Sometimes I've wondered if I was just selfish. Felt guilty sometimes, especially early on. But I knew it was right, too. I don't know. I was so young . . . afraid . . . confused."

Sam pulled her closer, and Maggie sobbed hard, resting her head on his shoulder.

"God! I haven't cried like that for years!" she said, wiping tears as she looked around the den. "I still think about it sometimes at the preschool. Wonder from time to time. 'What if?' When I'm comfortin' a cryin' child. Laughin' or singin' with 'em. Helpin' 'em learn."

"Oh, Maggie. You went alone?"

"Yeah. On the way over, asking myself, 'Are ya sure? What are ya doin'?' I had no idea how an abortion even happens. But I kept comin' back to my knowin'."

After staring long and hard into the fire's light, she looked up at Sam. "When I told my parents, it was a whole, hot mess. We worked through it. They worked through their own stuff. We came out of it okay."

"Oh my God, Maggie. I can only imagine."

The two, who knew of wrestling with stories past, stayed curled up on the couch, while Shadow did her best to lie at both of their feet.

Maggie took a deep breath and whispered, "I want to stay the night."

March 25, 2026
Morning of my Homecoming.
I see life now as a matter
of home. The soul leaves
its Source, its Home.
Mine, it seems, has
been searching for it
ever since.

21

Sam's Homecoming

SAM CAREFULLY GOT OUT OF BED in the morning, walked over to her side of their homecoming, and took in the beauty and magic of it all. Marveling at this lovely being who had come into his life.

By this time Shadow had come into the bedroom, lying on the floor on Maggie's side of the bed. She raised her head. Sam put out his hand, letting her know not to wake her.

He reached down to kiss Maggie's cheek. She stirred, turning to face him in her sleep.

Wondering how this all came to be, he thought of those awful days alone in his apartment. Of how the really good things in his life only needed his allowing. Not his forcing.

He remembered this angel telling him of her journaling, and how it had brought her healing. He knew it was now his time.

He quietly walked over to the den, where the McGee sisters once played long ago. An empty journal in hand that Maggie had given him . . . in case. Shadow quietly behind him all the way, resting her head on Sam's left foot. Offering one of her long, contented exhales.

He looked around again at that imagined library of his life, seeing the most recent arrival. The book about Maggie O'Brien and life's magic.

Opening to the blank page of Maggie's invitation, he took in all the grace that had come his way with a deep inhale. The words coming out as an exhale of pure wonder.

March 25, 2026

Morning of my homecoming.

I see life now as a matter of home.

The soul leaves its Source, its home. Mine, it seems, has been searching for it ever since. I must remember it. Know it at some innate level. Otherwise, why would I seek after it?

As a child I searched for home in a father whose door was never open.

I searched for it in the approval of a crowded gym.

I searched for home in a beautiful soul named Jadyn, expecting her to not only build it for me, but also to fill it with everything I thought I needed.

I first knew it in the open door of my mother's heart. Once inside, I saw that she was looking for it too.

I knew it in the embrace of my sister, Karen. My protector.

I've felt home most deeply in my love for my children, and in my longing to return there.

Avery has always been home for me. Standing at her open door, welcoming me no matter how I show up.

I've now returned home
In the arms of my father, while crying a lifetime of tears, in anger felt and released.
Compassion found. Forgiveness given and received.
Turns out, the story I always wanted from him was being written all along.

I've returned home again in Jadyn
In a hard-won gratitude for our life together. ALL of it.
In a love big enough now to embrace her truth.

With all my heart I hope I'm returning home with Ben, as we may be finding each other again, walking the path of vulnerability.

They say that when we die, our immigrant souls return to the home they left. I believe that. We truly are "just walking each other home," as Ram Dass taught.

Now I see that life itself has been walking me home.
Helping me remember it along the way.
In every light first seen in a required darkness
In every deep pain birthing an ever-deeper joy
In every feeling of separation bringing me to deeper connection
Every "no" discreetly leading to life's Yes!
Every feeling of guilt and shame met with grace
Every story and mystery holding its questions pointing the way
Every search telling me I'm already home.

Love, and all that was not Love: two sides of the same coin. Currency for the journey home.

Home lies now at my feet. This golden rescuer of mine.

Home lies in the room next to me. This soul known as Maggie. Bearing life's magic.

This is my homecoming.

My life.

Acknowledgments

So many wonderful people have walked with me on the journey of bringing this book home to its completion.

To my incredibly wise and beautiful wife, Doree, you are my Homecoming on this earth.

To my children, Sonja and Sarah, you are my ground.

To my sons-in-law, Jonathan and Luke, you are my support.

To my grandchildren, Soren and Olivia, you are my teachers.

To my walking buddy, Shadow, who pulled me along for fifteen years. You're still my guide. Happy adventures, girl.

To Bill Beaupre, whose artistry and spirituality make visual the sacred. william-beaupre.com

To Echo Bodine, who taught me to trust the Voice within as my most faithful companion.

To Melissa Anderson, whose initial editing and wisdom helped bring this book home to its intended truth.

To my soul sister, Sue Hein, who has walked with me through this Soul School of life.

To "The Sacred Circle of Beings," who together create space for renewal, honesty, challenge, laughter, and love.

To the readers of my column, I Remember Now, you walk with me on the road to remembering who and what we all are: Love. echobodine.com

To the wonderful people at Pen & Publish, I thank you.

www.ingramcontent.com/pod-product-compliance
Lightning Source LLC
Chambersburg PA
CBHW070756150726
48196CB00050B/1274
* 9 7 8 1 9 5 6 8 9 7 8 7 6 *